Piecemakers®

COUNTRY STORE

Costa Mesa, California USA

by the Piecemakers

That Patchwork Place®

Acknowledgments

First of all, we thank the Lord Jesus for leading and guiding us back to His Father, and for giving us the talents we needed to write this book. Second, we thank our customers, who have kept us in business. Lastly, we thank That Patchwork Place for printing our story.

All stories, poems, pen and ink drawings, and pattern designs are the original, unedited works of Piecemakers.

Credits

Editor-in-Chief . . . . Barbara Weiland
Managing Editor . . . . Greg Sharp
Text and Cover Design . . . . Kay Green
Typesetting . . . . Julianna Reynolds
Photography . . . . Brent Kane
Illustration and Graphics . . . . Laurel Strand
Stephanie Benson
Piecemakers

Piecemakers® Country Store
©1993 by Piecemakers

That Patchwork Place, Inc.
PO Box 118
Bothell, WA 98041-0118
USA

Printed in the United States of America
98 97 96 95 94 93   6 5 4 3 2

Piecemakers Country Store.
        p. cm. — (Quilt shop series)
     ISBN 1-56477-032-X :
     1. Patchwork—Patterns. 2. Quilting—Patterns. I. Series.
TT835.P55 1993
746.46—dc20   93-23168
                                                                CIP

Table of Contents

The Story of Piecemakers

A rainbow of fabrics and threads fills Piecemakers Country Store.

The country-kitchen room at Piecemakers.

Introduction

How do you describe a store that is the lifeblood of the people who run it? It is as cohesive as their unity of purpose and as diversified as the people themselves.

The foundation of Piecemakers Country Store is a group of pioneers who laid down everything—possessions, careers, hopes and dreams, and even their own lives—to follow Jesus Christ. He is the rock on which this foundation was built. The walls are the faith to build what we could not see. The people who walk through our doors when they open breathe new life into the store.

The patterns, stories, poems, recipes, and pictures found in this book are tangible evidence of a Creator we can't see, but who we know exists more surely than the book you hold in your hands. We hope you enjoy its contents and that it becomes a tool to tap creativity beyond your imagination!

4

Ka Ying marks quilting lines. Behind her are some of the many quilts the Piecemakers productions department has made to sell in the store.

The Beginning ...

The year was 1967. The Six Day War ended as abruptly as it began. The entire world seemed on the verge of an explosion. It was the decade of the sixties, and the world would never be the same again, for the Spirit of the Lord hovered over the waters of the deep and began birthing a new family of people. God had spoken, "Let there be light," and as He spoke, the light was separated from the darkness. Those who had ears to hear recognized the voice of their Savior and came forth from their slumber to follow Him. He gathered together those who would follow Him with a whole heart, fully committed to Him, willing to lay down their lives and become His will in the earth.

After approximately ten years of fellowship and seeking God's will for their lives, some of the women decided to make cloth items. We took our meager works to the fair, and lo and behold, all sold, and we saw a need in the community that we could fill. With six willing-to-work handmaidens, six bolts of fabric, and some needles and thread, Piecemakers' flag began to unfurl, although at that time we were still without a name.

What shall we call this unknown entity that was taking form? As we sat one day brainstorming for a name, these came to mind: "The Comforter," "Sew & Sew," and "Pieces and Patches." One man said, "This child shall be called "Piecemakers," and the women and men all said, "Amen!" The very next weekend, four eager quilters headed for a quilt show in Oregon with their handmade creations in the back of the van. They spotted a bumper sticker that said, "Blessed are the quilters, for they shall be called Piecemakers." They knew without a doubt that Piecemakers would be the name of the new baby that was being birthed.

The quilt fair in Oregon was encouraging, as everything sold readily. It is always a good feeling to leave a show empty-handed. The love for creating and making things was so satisfying that we were instilled with the desire to encourage others to begin creating. Sharing the newfound joy of creating with others was the beginning of our school. I suppose in early America, when we were still wonderfully innocent, that desire to share was the beginning of passing on skills and learning.

Students move in for a closer look at a demonstration of silk-ribbon embroidery techniques.

The potpourri branch of the Piecemakers tree is located in the loft of the warehouse, where jars of flowers decorate the shelves and the aroma of oils and spices fills the air.

In the one thousand nine hundred and seventy-eighth year of our Lord, Piecemakers was formed into a corporation. Money has always been a by-product of working at Piecemakers Country Store, never a priority. Because Piecemakers store belongs to the people, our growth has always been the result of fulfilling the desires of those we serve.

Piecemakers began to blossom like a rose, with our fragrance reaching around the world. In 1988, we put out our first calendar with twelve quilt blocks and patterns. I was in Wisconsin when that offspring was born, and a copy was sent to me. When I opened the package in the mailbox, the beauty of it brought a lump to my throat. Presently, our yearly calendar graces the walls of friends in countries throughout the world. The calendar was the firstborn of things published. Soon our patterns, books (including a cookbook), and Piecemakers fabric found their way into the homes of not only people in this country, but people in other lands as well.

Two men instrumental in our continuing growth are Sandy Schner and John Simonsen. They come into the store regularly to visit and suggest we do this and that. Their faith in us continues to prompt us to try new adventures. Around 1986, we began having our very own needles manufactured. Because there is no needle factory in America, we went abroad and now have unique, Japanese-standard needles created exclusively for Piecemakers.

As God continued to draw those whom He desired to walk in His works and His ways, the men came and joined the women because they, too, wanted to get back to grassroots living. The men also work with their hands—tilers, bricklayers, and construction workers with their contractor's license— each man individually desiring to have God's will first and foremost in his life.

Day to Day ...

New ideas are continually being birthed at Piecemakers. We always feel rather honored if people copy what we do. We never forbid taking pictures in the store or drinking from our well of creativity.

At the present time, we have 300 classes every three months, turning out over twelve thousand students per year with no government subsidy. We are not nonprofit. We "give to Caesar that which is Caesar's, and to God that which is God's." A quarterly class schedule going to some twenty thousand people is three dollars for a year's subscription.

Currently, one of the most rewarding experiences is seeing the big tour buses drive up to bring people from all walks of life to spend a day with us. Our tours all include a delicious lunch and a half hour of getting acquainted as the "Piecemakers Country Singers"

The old-fashioned candy counter is a favorite spot for kids of all ages.

make everyone feel "down home" with their fresh country singing. We have door prizes and a mini fashion show to introduce some of the lines of clothing we sell in our boutique called "The Fig Leaf." We talk about our beginnings and how we grew, and after a half hour of getting acquainted, we have the store tour and then lunch.

Four times a year, in April, July, October, and December, we have a festival featuring 150 artisans who are, without question, the most original crafters in all of America. What fun it is to see these grassroots pioneering men and women drive up with their precious cargo! The parking lot is a buzz of activity as each crafter busily works to set up his booth and prepare for the throngs that now come to these festivals.

Piecemakers Country Singers perform at all the major Piecemakers events.

In Piecemakers millinery classes, students can learn to shape and decorate hats for every occasion.

There is country singing, lots of food, walking puppeteers, the Newport Beach Birdman, homemade pies, and popcorn. You name it—our craft fairs have it.

Early in the morning of the fair, the parking lot is teeming with activity. Coffee and coffee cake tide the workers over until the food booths begin to open. Beef sandwiches, hot dogs, baked potatoes, salad, yogurt—there is food for all. The Piecemakers' apple pie is a special drawing card. People come from all over just to have the pie that tastes like Grandma used to make. The recipe appears on page 32 of this book.

The daily routine at Piecemakers is always comforting. Our extended family is made up of the people who walk through our front door and give us the pleasure of serving them. We are very aware of the fact that without them we are nothing.

Once a year, in the first part of January, we have a Sunrise Fabric Sale with 40% off on all fabric from 6:00 a.m. to 7:00 a.m.; 30% off from 7:00 to 8:00, and 20% off from 8:00 to 9:00. Women are just plain fun!

Before dawn they are out standing in line, enjoying talking with one another. For next year, we are planning a breakfast for all the early risers.

We celebrate Easter weekend with a pet parade. Instead of showing off our clothes we show off our pets. What fun it is to see these little animals put on their best faces.

Twice a year we have a Fashion Show—not like any other fashion show, as the models are the staff you meet when you come into the store. The apparel world is almost as exciting as the quilt world. I never cease to admire the designers who bring forth new fashions, new fabrics, and fun clothes for young and old, at prices everyone can afford.

Visitors enjoy the many activities at a Piecemakers Craft Fair.

There's something for everyone at the fair.

About the kids ...

I think a special section should be dedicated to the precious cargo God put into our care—the children. We have a wide variety of kids' classes, especially during vacation time. We also have birthday parties where each guest creates something to take home.

Once a year, on Christmas Eve, we have Kids' Demo Day (D-Day). Each child signs up for the day and goes from one classroom to another, making items to take home as Christmas gifts or decorations.

Let us pray, as each baby is born into the world, that we bear the burden of responsibility in nurturing what we bring forth. Let's all work together to help young parents with that responsibility. Lord, give us patience and Your nurturing love for children all over the world, that love which prefers the welfare of our offspring over the fulfilling of our own selfish desires.

About the staff ...

It would take more than a book to really tell of the precious life of each diligent member of our staff. We have the immediate family, the original members who have clung together during some pretty tough times. Then we have dedicated people who have joined us and sheltered us from the storm when all seemed dark. They were there to encourage in good times and in bad times. To call them employees would be blasphemous. These people are bone of our bone and flesh of our flesh.

Included in this group of loyal people are seventy-five teachers, our quilters, our production personnel, and our very loyal family members from Russia, Laos, and Mexico. For all these friends, we give thanks to the Lord. And to each of you, dear reader, we pray God's blessings—that His mercy heal you in sorrowful times and His joy continue to be your strength.

Things are "looking up"—our Piecemakers family.

General Directions

Preshrink and press all fabrics before cutting them. Use ¼"-wide seam allowances unless otherwise specified. Note that the yardages given for binding fabric will yield 2½"-wide bias strips that finish to approximately ⅜".

For a primitive, old-fashioned look, you may want to "tea dye" your fabrics. For one yard of fabric, bring six quarts of water to a boil. Add two family-size tea bags or six regular tea bags. Simmer five to ten minutes to get the tea water the desired color. Remove tea bags. Wet the fabric before immersing it in the boiling tea. This helps the fabric to absorb the color better. Simmer about ten minutes. Dry the fabric in the dryer and press.

Some patterns in this book call for embroidery stitches to be used as embellishments.

Tools and Supplies

You will need the following basic quiltmaking supplies to make the projects in this book.

General Quiltmaking Supplies

Rotary cutter, cutting mat, and 6"-wide acrylic ruler

Scissors for cutting fabric and paper

Small embroidery scissors for hand appliqué

Marking pencils for light and dark fabrics

Template plastic

Straight pins

Quilter's disc or Quilter's Quarter ruler

Piecemakers' needles for hand appliqué, embroidery needles for decorative stitches

Embroidery floss

Thread in neutral color for piecing, and in matching colors for hand appliqué and binding

¼" and ⅜" bias bars (optional)

Supplies for Hand Quilting

Piecemakers' needles—milliners' for basting, betweens for quilting

Thimble

Quilting hoop or frame

Quilting thread

¼"-wide masking tape

Quilting stencils

Supplies for Hand Tying

Chenille needle

DMC Perle Cotton thread, size 3

Needle grabber—purchase one, or use a balloon or thick rubber band

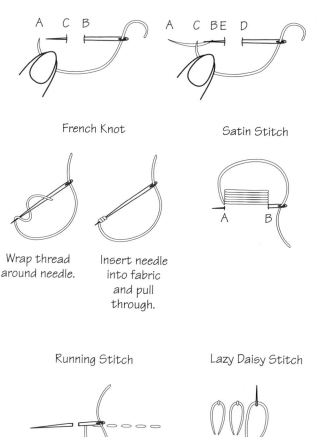

Stem Stitch

French Knot

Wrap thread around needle.

Insert needle into fabric and pull through.

Satin Stitch

Running Stitch

Lazy Daisy Stitch

Piecing

Making and Using Templates for Machine Piecing

1. Trace templates onto template plastic and cut exactly on the drawn line.
2. Place template on wrong side of fabric.* Draw around template with a soft lead pencil.

   *When the template says "reversed," *flip* the template over to draw around it.

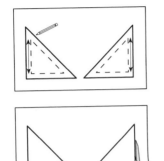

Stitching the Pieces Together

1. Pin pieces right sides together with raw edges even.

2. To machine piece, stitch ¼" from the raw edges, with the machine set for 12 to 15 stitches to the inch.

   If you prefer hand piecing, use a small running stitch and begin and end stitching ¼" from raw edges.
3. Press seams to one side. Press seams that will meet at intersections in opposite directions to eliminate excess thickness.

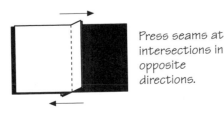

Press seams at intersections in opposite directions.

Appliqué

The word "appliqué" is a French word that means "to apply." When you appliqué, you "apply" different fabric shapes onto a background fabric to form a design or picture.

1. Trace patterns onto template plastic and cut exactly on the drawn line.
2. Trace around all templates on the right side of the fabric. This is the sewing line.
3. Cut fabric a scant ¼" outside the traced lines. You do not need to measure this seam allowance, just "eye" it.

4. Before sewing the appliqué pieces onto the background fabric, you may need to mark the placement of the design. Tape the pattern to a sunny window or light box. Center the background fabric right side up on top of the pattern and tape fabric in place. Trace just inside the design lines with a very light pencil line so the marks won't show later.
5. Clip curves to almost, but not through, the sewing lines. Clipping enables you to turn under the seam allowance of the appliqué piece without forming puckers.

Don't clip straight areas or the tip.

6. For hand appliqué, we recommend a Piecemakers hand appliqué needle, or a #10 or #12 quilting needle. A fine needle gives you tiny, smooth stitches. You may need to use a needle-threader for these small needles, but it is worth it for the quality of work you'll get. Avoid big, fat needles.
7. Quilt plan diagrams are included for each quilt. Study the diagram to see which pieces must be sewn in place first. Always work from the background to the foreground.

Lay the first piece to be appliquéd in place on the background. To line up the piece, stick a pin through some point on your drawn line and stick it through to the corresponding point on the background. Repeat pinning through at least one more point. Baste in place.

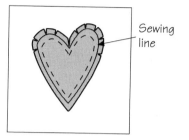

Sewing line

8. Thread your needle with an 18" length of thread to match the appliqué piece. Tie a knot in one end. Using a blindstitch, appliqué the piece in place. To blindstitch, fold seam allowance under with your needle, rolling the pencil line slightly underneath. Bring the needle from the back to the front, catching the fold. Next, push the needle back down into the background fabric directly beside the place where it came up. Take an extra blind stitch at the beginning. Anchor about 1" of your folded seam allowance with your thumb as you stitch.

Take a ⅛"-long stitch underneath the background fabric and come up, catching the edge of the fold again. Repeat. Add each piece in order, using matching thread colors. Edges that will be over-lapped by another appliqué piece should be left unsewn to avoid excess thickness in the finished work.

Making Yo-yos

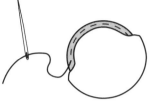

Little fabric circles, gathered to resemble a child's yo-yo, are easy to make and add a dimensional embel-lishment to your quilt top. Make them out of fabric scraps.

1. Cut a circle of fabric, using one of the pattern pieces.
2. With the wrong side of the fabric facing you, hand baste a ⅛" to ¼" seam allowance all around, leaving the tails of thread.
3. Pull the basting stitches up until the circle forms a little pouch. Centering the gathered edge, flatten it into a circle.

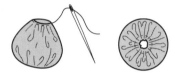

4. Secure the threads underneath the gathering or tie off on the back of the yo-yo.

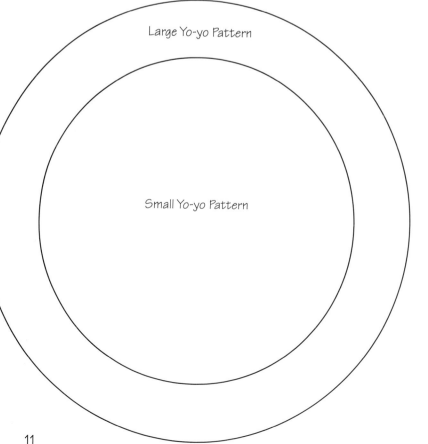

Large Yo-yo Pattern

Small Yo-yo Pattern

Adding Borders

Cut border strips from selvage to selvage, across the fabric width, as instructed in each pattern. To make border strips long enough for each side of your quilt, sew the cut strips together. Some of the quilt patterns have mitered corners on the borders while others have straight-cut corners.

To attach borders with straight-cut corners:

1. Measure the width of the quilt at the center and cut two border strips to that measurement.

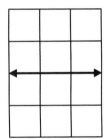

Measure width
at center.

2. Fold the quilt in half lengthwise and mark centers of top and bottom with pins. Repeat with the two border strips.
3. Pin borders to top and bottom, matching centers and ends. Stitch the borders to the quilt, easing to fit as needed. Press seams toward the borders.

Note: One or both outside edges of the quilt may not be the same measurement as the center of the quilt. Cutting both borders exactly the same length as the center, then easing to fit as needed, makes the quilt come out square.

4. Measure the length of the quilt top plus top and bottom borders, and cut two border strips to that length. Attach borders to the sides as described for top and bottom borders.

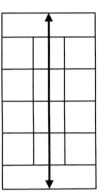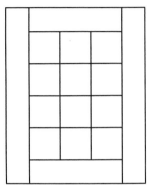

Measure length at center
after adding top and
bottom borders.

To attach borders with mitered corners:

Note: If your quilt has mitered multiple borders, sew all border strips for each side of the quilt to each other, before attaching them to the quilt top.

1. Find the center of the border strip and the center of one side of the quilt. Pin the border strip to the quilt with right sides together and centers matching.
2. Beginning ¼" from the corner, sew the border to the quilt top, using a ¼"-wide seam allowance. Stop sewing ¼" from the opposite end. Be sure to backstitch when you begin and end stitching. Sew each strip to the quilt top in the same manner.

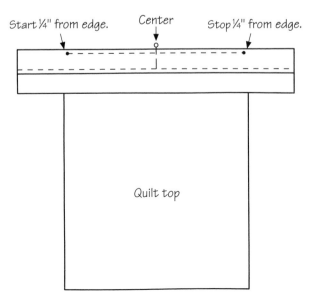

3. Press the borders toward the edge of the quilt. Turn the quilt wrong side up and straighten borders as shown.

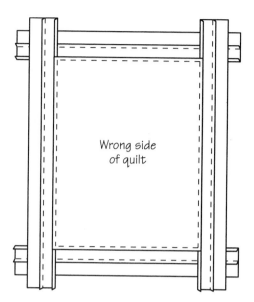

Wrong side of quilt

4. Working with one corner at a time, fold a corner diagonally, lining up adjacent border strips. Place the 45° line of the ruler along the top edge of the border. Place the edge of the ruler at the point where the border attaches to the quilt. Draw a line along this edge of the ruler on the quilt border.

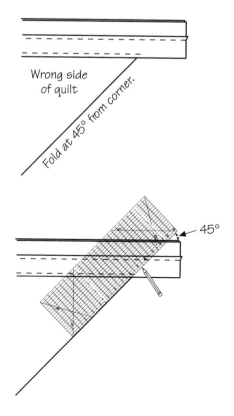

Wrong side of quilt

Fold at 45° from corner.

45°

5. Pin where the border seams meet each other. Sew on the drawn line, being careful not to catch the corner of the quilt top. This seam is a 45° angle from the corner of the quilt.

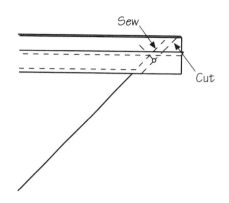

Sew

Cut

6. Trim excess border fabric, leaving a ½"-wide seam allowance. Press seam open.

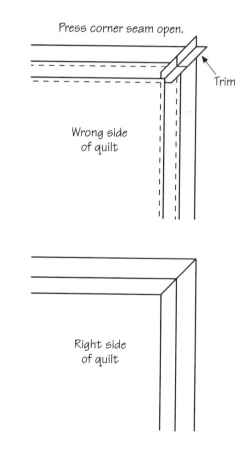

Press corner seam open.

Trim

Wrong side of quilt

Right side of quilt

Quilt Finishing

Prepare the quilt top for hand quilting by marking the quilting design on the top with a fabric marking pencil. Decide where you will quilt the individual pieces. Quilt in-the-ditch around the pieces or quilt ¼" away from the seams. Larger areas lend themselves nicely to a more elaborate quilting design.

Preparing the Quilt Layers

1. Make the "quilt sandwich" by taping the backing fabric, wrong side up, to a table or to the floor. Make sure the backing is pulled taut. Center the batting on top of the backing. Place the quilt top right side up on the batting.
2. Pinning from the center of the quilt out to the edges, continually smooth the layers. If you will be tying the quilt, pinning the layers together should be sufficient, so you can skip step 3.
3. If you plan on quilting by hand, baste the layers together. Use a long needle and thread to hand baste with large stitches, from the center of the quilt out to the edges. Space stitches no more than 6" apart and make stitches 1" to 2" long. Do not pull the stitches tight or the top will pucker.

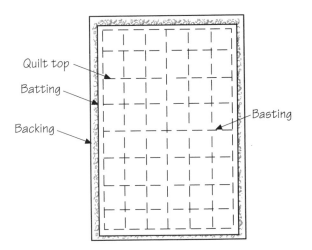

Quilt top
Batting
Backing
Basting

Quilting By Hand

1. To hand quilt, use a very short quilting needle to get the best leverage for your stitches. (We recommend a #9, #10, or a #12 between needle—the higher the number, the smaller the needle.) Using an 18" length of quilting thread, tie a single knot in one end. Hide the knot by sewing into the

top and pulling it gently into the batting. Take a tiny backstitch to secure the knot. Begin in the center of the quilt and work out to the edges.

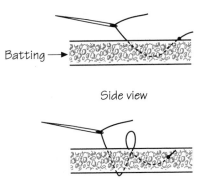

Batting

Side view

2. Load your needle with at least three or four stitches at a time and quilt, using a small running stitch.

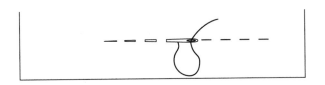

3. To end a thread, tie two or three single knots near the needle, take a small backstitch, and pull the thread gently into the batting to hide the knots. Clip the thread at the surface of the quilt.

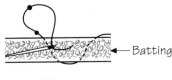

Batting

Side view

Tying the Quilt

Tying a quilt can be a wonderful alternative to quilting when you want results in a hurry. Use DMC Perle Cotton #3 and a chenille needle. A "needle grabber" is also helpful. Use a thick rubber band or a balloon to grip the needle when pulling it through the layers of fabric.

1. Thread a chenille needle with a long length of perle cotton. Double the thread, but do not tie a knot. Run the thread through several areas to be tied, sewing through all three layers.

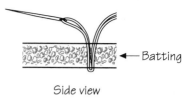

Side view

2. When you come to the end of the thread in your needle, leave enough of a thread tail for tying. Clip between the stitches, leaving the long thread tails.

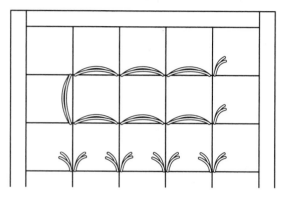

3. Tie the threads, beginning by tying once, just like you are tying your shoe. Next, tie again, but loop the thread through twice. Pull tight. When all threads are tied, trim tails to approximately 1" lengths.

Loop ends through twice.

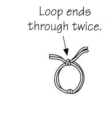

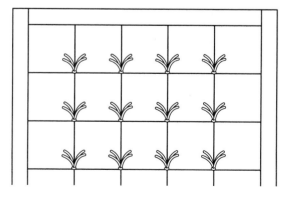

Binding

There are several methods for preparing and attaching quilt binding. We prefer binding cut on the bias grain. Measure around the quilt to determine the required length of binding. It may be necessary to piece strips together.

1. Cut bias strips 2½" wide. Seam pieces together at a 45° angle as shown. To cut a bias strip on the true bias grain of your fabric, start in a corner next to a selvage edge, if possible. Use a ruler to mark 6" from the corner on each side. Connect these marks to draw a diagonal line. Draw a parallel line 2½" away to make your first bias strip. Continue drawing parallel lines until you have enough binding strips to go around the edges of your quilt.

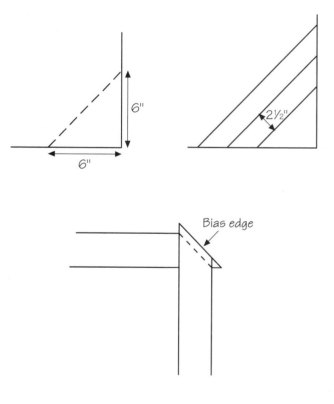

2. Fold the binding strip in half, wrong sides together, and press. Stitch through both layers ¼" from the raw edges.

3. Trim the quilt batting and backing even with the quilt top. If the quilt won't be quilted right up to the unfinished edge, baste around the edges to keep them from shifting.

4. Stitch the binding to the quilt, beginning in the middle of one side. Match the raw edges of the binding to the raw edge of the quilt. Leave about 5" of binding hanging free at the beginning and fold the excess binding at an angle as shown.

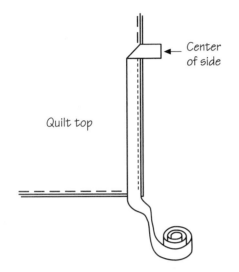

Center of side

Quilt top

5. Stitch the binding to the quilt, using a ¼"-wide seam allowance and ending ¼" from the raw edge at the corner. Backstitch and cut the threads. Do not cut the binding.

6. Form a pleat in the binding at the corner. Leaving the pleat free from the stitching, pivot the quilt and sew ¼" from the corner as before. Repeat around the remaining sides and corners of the quilt.

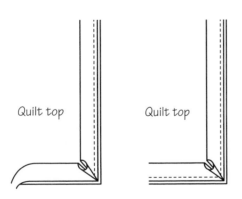

Quilt top   Quilt top

7. Overlap the tail of binding fabric where you began sewing. Trim excess binding tail even with the edge of the quilt.

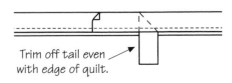

Trim off tail even with edge of quilt.

8. Turn the binding to the back of the quilt and blindstitch in place just over the machine-stitching line. The corners will form a mitered pleat automatically when the binding is turned.

Adding a Hanging Sleeve

Sew a sleeve of fabric to the back of the quilt if you plan to hang it on a wall.

1. Measure the width of the quilt and cut a 4½"-wide strip of fabric that length. Turn under ¼" at each short end and stitch.

Hanging sleeve

2. Fold the fabric in half lengthwise, wrong sides together. Sew the raw edges together, using a ¼"-wide seam allowance. Leave both ends of the sleeve open.

3. Press the seam so it is centered on one side of the sleeve.

4. With the top edge of the sleeve against the back of the quilt just below the binding, hand sew along the top and bottom edges of the sleeve.

5. Insert a wooden dowel into the sleeve. Hang on nails or cup hooks inserted into the wall.

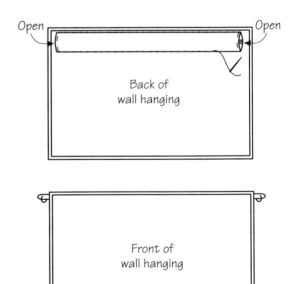

Open   Open

Back of wall hanging

Front of wall hanging

Grandma's Garden Gate

Finished size: 38½" x 38½"   Quilt Plan

Colorful flowers of all shapes and sizes wind around the garden trellis. This beautiful garden beckons viewers to sit down and rest for a while. The yo-yo and button embellishments add a special dimension to the appliqués.

Color photo on page 37.

Materials: 44"-wide fabric

¼ yd. green for grass

1 yd. blue for sky

1 yd. white for fence and trellis

¼ yd. each of 2 greens and
1 brown for stems and leaves

¼ yd. yellow for sunflowers

⅛ yd. brown print for sunflower centers*

⅛ yd. each of 6 fabrics for flowers (Refer to the color
photograph of the quilt on page 37.)

½ yd. pink for border

1¼ yds. for backing

42½" x 42½" piece of batting

⅔ yd. for binding

2 pieces blue, each 6" x 7½", for bird

6" x 7½" piece of batting for bird

2 pieces, each 4" x 4", of contrasting
fabric for bird wing

4" x 4" piece of batting for bird wing

Embroidery floss in medium brown for vines

2 or 3 old buttons

Small bead for bird's eye

*The 6 purple flowers, the dark blue and pink flowers,
and 2 of the sunflowers need yo-yo centers.
These may be cut from assorted fabric scraps.

Cutting for Pieced Background

*Cut all strips across the fabric
width (selvage to selvage).*

From the green, cut:
2 strips, each 2½" wide, for the grass

From the blue, cut:
1 strip, 2½" wide, for the sky
1 strip, 3½" wide, for the sky
1 strip, 1½" wide for the sky; crosscut into
22 squares, each 1½" x 1½"
1 strip, 19½" x 32½", for the sky background

From the white, cut:
2 strips, each 2½" x 42", for the horizontal fence rails
1 strip, 11½" x 42"; crosscut into 11 pieces,
each 2½" wide, for the fence pickets
Enough 2½"-wide bias strips to make a piece
47" long for the trellis*

*Seam bias strips together as shown.
Trim seams to ¼" and press to one side.

From the pink, cut:
4 strips, each 3½" wide, for the border.

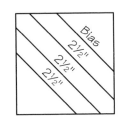

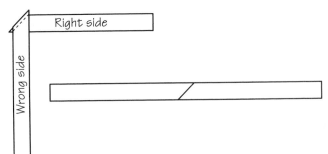

Directions

Background

1. Using ¼"-wide seam allowances, sew strips together as shown.

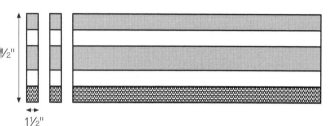

Sky – 2½" x 42"
Fence – 2½" x 42"
Sky – 3½" x 42"
Fence – 2½" x 42"
Grass – 2½" x 42"

2. Cut this set of strips into 10 rectangles, each 1½" x 11½".

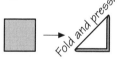

1½"

3. Fold the 1½" squares of sky fabric diagonally with wrong sides together. Press.

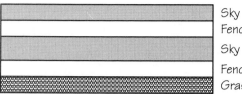

Fold and press.

4. With right sides together, place a 1½" square on the upper right corner of a 2½" x 11½" picket fence rectangle. Sew on the crease. Place another 1½" creased square on the upper left corner of the same picket and sew on the crease. Trim off the upper pieces of the sky fabric, leaving a ¼"-wide seam allowance. *Do not cut the picket fabric.* Turn the sky pieces out and press. Repeat these steps for all 11 fence pickets.

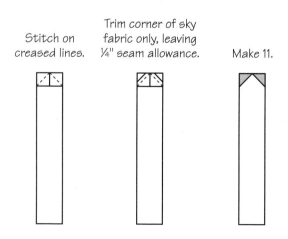

Stitch on creased lines.

Trim corner of sky fabric only, leaving ¼" seam allowance.

Make 11.

5. Sew the 11 picket fence units to the 10 sky/fence units.

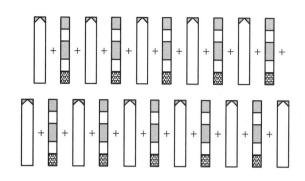

6. Add the sky and grass strips to the fence unit.

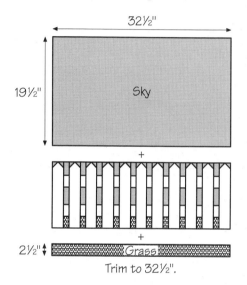

32½"

19½"

Sky

2½" ↕ Grass

Trim to 32½".

7. To make the trellis, fold a 2½"-wide bias strip in half lengthwise with wrong sides together. Sew along raw edges, using a ¼"-wide seam allowance.

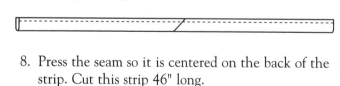

8. Press the seam so it is centered on the back of the strip. Cut this strip 46" long.

46"

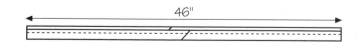

9. Baste by hand or machine along the middle 20" of one edge of the strip. Draw up basting slightly to gather this section of the trellis strip. The gathered section is the inside edge of the trellis.

10. Pin 1 trellis end to the inside corner of the third picket from the right side; pin the remaining trellis end to the inside corner of the third picket from the left side. Turn under the raw edge at each end of the trellis. Hand stitch ends in place. Pin the trellis to the quilt background, easing in the fullness as needed. Do not appliqué the trellis yet.

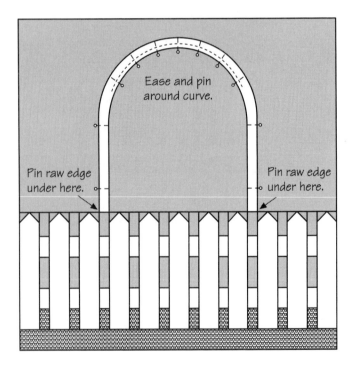

Ease and pin around curve.

Pin raw edge under here.

Pin raw edge under here.

Appliqué

Templates on pullout pattern insert.

Use the quilt plan on page 17 as a reference for this free-flowing design. Follow the instructions on pages 10–11 for cutting and sewing all the appliqués except the bird.

1. Use contrasting colors of fabric for the bird and the wing. Place two 6" x 7½" fabric pieces, right sides together, for the bird's body. Trace the bird body pattern onto the top piece of fabric. Stack these pieces on top of the 6" x 7½" piece of batting.

2. Sew exactly on the lines, leaving an opening for turning. Cut out the bird's body, leaving a ¼"-wide seam allowance all around. Clip the curves and turn bird's body right side out.

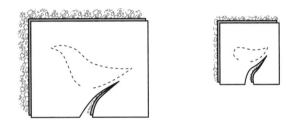

3. Repeat these steps for the bird's wing, using two 4" x 4" pieces of fabric and the 4" x 4" piece of batting. Hand stitch the openings closed. Tack the wing to the bird. Add a button or a bead for the bird's eye.

4. Cutting only a few pieces at a time, cut 1"-wide bias strips for green and brown stems. Cut more stems as you need them. To make longer stems, join the strips together as needed, using ¼"-wide seam allowances.

5. Fold each stem strip in half lengthwise, wrong sides together. Sew along the raw edge, using a scant ¼"-wide seam allowance. Press the seam so it is centered on the back of the strip.* Trim seam if necessary.

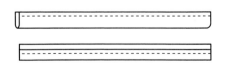

*Use a ¼"-wide bias bar to simplify pressing the stem strips. Insert the bar inside the strip, pushing it through as you press until it comes out the other end.

6. Refer to the quilt plan to pin and baste the flowers, stems, and leaves in place. Work from the background to the foreground. Cut the stem strips the necessary lengths. Tuck the ends of the shorter stems under the longer ones.

7. Appliqué the pieces in place as basted. Leave 2 of the leaf appliqués hanging free on each side of the quilt top until after the border is attached. Sew the bird in place, leaving its head and tail free.

Finishing

1. With 3 strands of embroidery floss, embroider the vines with the stem stitch.
2. Make yo-yos for flower centers. See page 11 for yo-yo templates and directions. Tack the yo-yos in the center of each flower with several hand stitches.
3. Measure the quilt for straight-cut borders as shown on page 12. Sew the top and bottom border strips to the quilt top, then add the side borders.
4. Appliqué the remaining leaf edges to the border.
5. Finish your quilt, following the quilt-finishing directions on page 14–16.

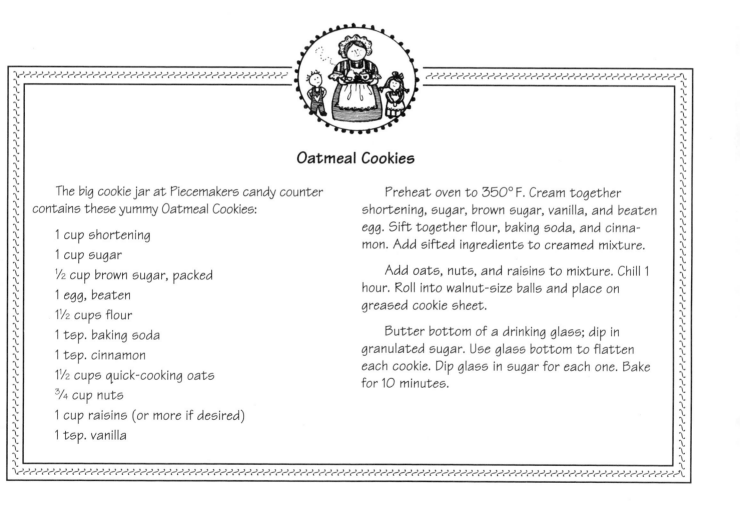

Oatmeal Cookies

The big cookie jar at Piecemakers candy counter contains these yummy Oatmeal Cookies:

1 cup shortening
1 cup sugar
½ cup brown sugar, packed
1 egg, beaten
1½ cups flour
1 tsp. baking soda
1 tsp. cinnamon
1½ cups quick-cooking oats
¾ cup nuts
1 cup raisins (or more if desired)
1 tsp. vanilla

Preheat oven to 350° F. Cream together shortening, sugar, brown sugar, vanilla, and beaten egg. Sift together flour, baking soda, and cinnamon. Add sifted ingredients to creamed mixture.

Add oats, nuts, and raisins to mixture. Chill 1 hour. Roll into walnut-size balls and place on greased cookie sheet.

Butter bottom of a drinking glass; dip in granulated sugar. Use glass bottom to flatten each cookie. Dip glass in sugar for each one. Bake for 10 minutes.

These are the things that ye shall do; speak ye every man the truth to his neighbor; execute the judgment of truth and peace in your gates. Zechariah 8:16

Mr. Grogan's Garden

Finished size: 29" x 36"   Quilt Plan

Since the beginning of time, gardens have offered inspiration and a place of rest for the soul.

In this popular meeting place for friends, you can almost smell the flowers that grow along the fence. "Mr. Grogan's Garden" is a companion quilt to "Grandma's Garden Gate," page 17. You'll want to make both wall hangings!

Color photo on page 38.

Materials: 44"-wide fabric

⅓ yd. each of 2 fabrics for fence*

⅛ yd. for ground

½ yd. for sky

¼ yd. each of 4 fabrics for stems and leaves

¼ yd. for sunflowers

⅛ yd. each (or scraps) of 6 assorted fabrics for flowers

½ yd. for 3" border

1 yd. for backing

⅔ yd. for binding

33" x 39" piece of batting

Old buttons, small doilies, and assorted scraps for yo-yo flower centers.

* One fabric should be slightly darker than the other. If using directional prints, you will need ½ yd. of each.

Cutting for Pieced Background

Cut all strips across the fabric width (selvage to selvage).

All measurements include ¼"-wide seam allowances. Cut the grass, sky, and fence pieces as listed below.
1 ground piece - 2½" x 30½"
1 sky piece - 7½" x 30½"

Cut the remaining pieces, using the templates as required.
9 sky pieces - Template A
2 sky pieces - Template B
5 fence pieces - each 3½" x 12½" of first color
5 fence pieces - each 3½" x 12½" of second color
5 Template A - from first fence color
5 Template A - from second fence color

Directions

1. Sew the 3½" x 12½" fence pieces together, alternating the two colors.

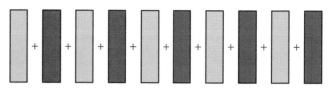

2. Sew the sky and fence triangles (Template A) together to make a long strip. Sew B and Br pieces to the ends of the strip. These triangles tend to stretch a bit when sewn, so don't worry if you have to ease them a little. When the strip is complete, it will look like this:

▽+△+▽+▲+▽+△+▽+▲+▽+△+▽+▲+▽+△+▽+▲+▽+△+▽+△+▽
△△△△△△△△△△

3. Sew the sky, fence/sky strip, fence, and ground together as shown.

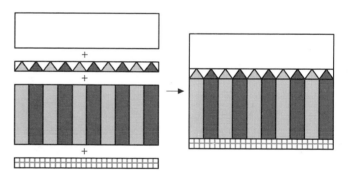

Appliqué

Templates on pullout pattern insert.

Since Mr. Grogan's Garden is a free-flowing design, your placement of the appliqués may vary. Use the quilt plan on page 22 as a reference. Refer to pages 10–11 for cutting and sewing the appliqué pattern pieces.

1. On the bias grain of the fabric, cut 1"-wide strips* for the flower stems.

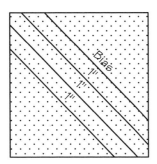

*Since sunflower stems are usually thicker than the stems of other flowers, cut these bias strips 1¼" wide.

Don't cut all your fabric at this time. You can cut more stems as you need them. To make longer stems, join the strips together, using ¼"-wide seam allowances.

2. Fold each stem strip in half lengthwise, wrong sides together. Stitch a scant ¼" from the raw edges. Press the seam so it is centered on the back of the strip.** Trim seam if necessary.

** Use a ¼"-wide bias bar to simplify the pressing. Insert the bar inside the strip, pushing the bar through as you press the stem until it comes out the other end. You will need a ⅜"-wide bias bar for the wider sunflower stem strips.

3. Appliqué all the stems to the quilt background. Cut the stem strips to get the necessary lengths as you go. When basting stems in place, be sure to tuck the shorter stems under the longer ones.

4. Appliqué the leaves and flowers to the quilt top in any order you wish, sewing the flower centers on last. See below.

Finishing

1. Make the flower centers with buttons, yo-yos, and small doilies. For the yo-yo flower bush, make 4 large yo-yos and 7 small yo-yos. To make yo-yos, refer to page 11 for yo-yo templates and instructions.

2. Cut 4 border strips, each 3½" wide, cutting across the fabric width (selvage to selvage). Refer to pages 12–13 in the general directions for making mitered corners on the border pieces.

3. Finish your wall hanging, following the quilt-finishing directions on pages 14–16.

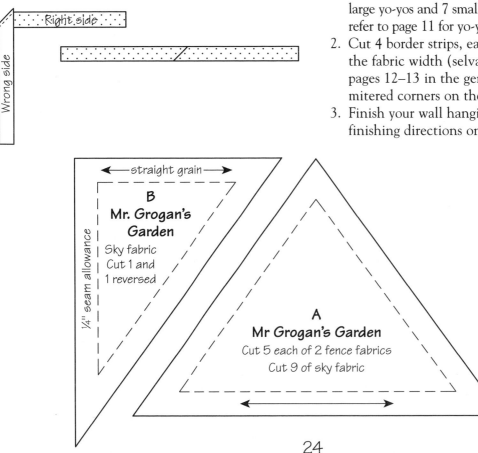

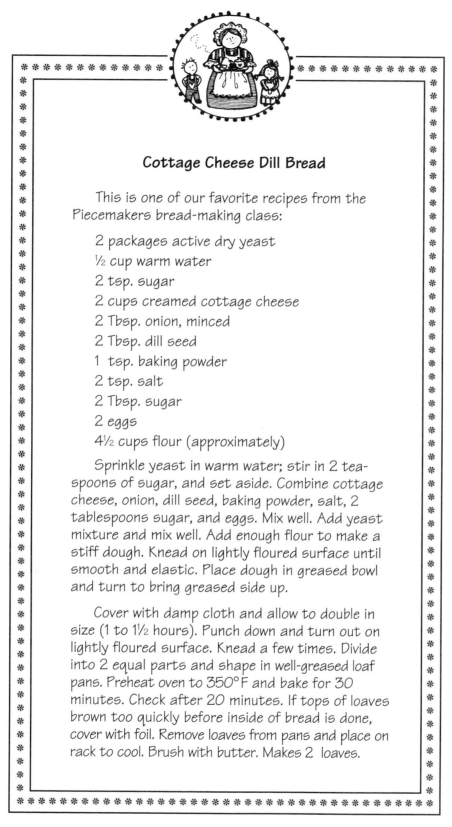

Cottage Cheese Dill Bread

This is one of our favorite recipes from the Piecemakers bread-making class:

2 packages active dry yeast
½ cup warm water
2 tsp. sugar
2 cups creamed cottage cheese
2 Tbsp. onion, minced
2 Tbsp. dill seed
1 tsp. baking powder
2 tsp. salt
2 Tbsp. sugar
2 eggs
4½ cups flour (approximately)

Sprinkle yeast in warm water; stir in 2 teaspoons of sugar, and set aside. Combine cottage cheese, onion, dill seed, baking powder, salt, 2 tablespoons sugar, and eggs. Mix well. Add yeast mixture and mix well. Add enough flour to make a stiff dough. Knead on lightly floured surface until smooth and elastic. Place dough in greased bowl and turn to bring greased side up.

Cover with damp cloth and allow to double in size (1 to 1½ hours). Punch down and turn out on lightly floured surface. Knead a few times. Divide into 2 equal parts and shape in well-greased loaf pans. Preheat oven to 350°F and bake for 30 minutes. Check after 20 minutes. If tops of loaves brown too quickly before inside of bread is done, cover with foil. Remove loaves from pans and place on rack to cool. Brush with butter. Makes 2 loaves.

For as the earth bringeth forth her bud, and as the garden causeth the things that are sown in it to spring forth; so the Lord God will cause righteousness and praise to spring forth before all the nations. Isaiah 61:11

An Apple for Teacher

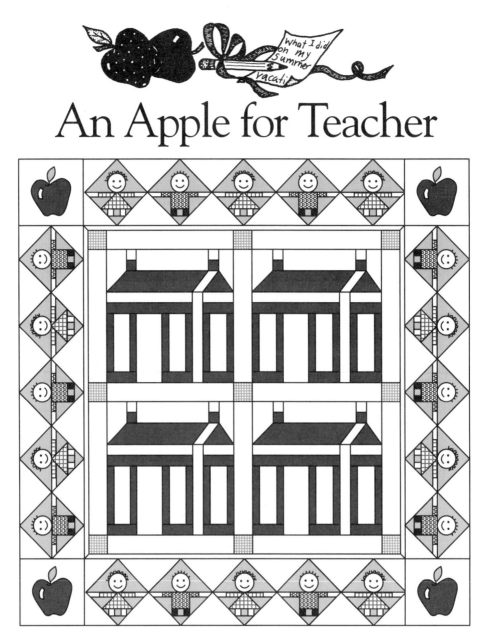

Finished size: 49" x 49"   Quilt Plan

Boys, girls, and apples surrounding primitive schoolhouses bring back memories of small-town America not so long ago. As a child, I visited a two-room schoolhouse with my grandmother in the backwoods of Alabama. Grandmother taught first through third grades around a pot-bellied stove on frosty mornings. In front of the blackboard, a shiny red apple sat on the rough-hewn teacher's desk.

"An Apple for Teacher" is based on a Piecemakers pattern-of-the-month, designed for September 1987. The quilt combines traditional patchwork with the primitive look that is popular today. The apples and the children's faces provide a soft touch of appliqué. Each child's face may be embroidered differently to reflect individual personalities.

Color photo on page 40.

Materials: 44"-wide fabric

½ yd. red for schoolhouses

1½ yds. cream for schoolhouses, background, inner border, and background in kids' border

½ yd. green for lattice

⅛ yd. plaid for cornerstones

1 yd. tan for background in kids' blocks and apple blocks

¼ yd. blue for boys' shirt and pants

¼ yd. blue plaid for girls' dresses

¼ yd. cream for children's faces and arms

¼ yd. red for apples

Assorted red and green scraps for leaves and windows on apples

Assorted colors of embroidery floss for children's hair, facial features, and apple stems

53" x 53" piece of batting

3 yds. for backing

¾ yd. green for binding

Schoolhouse Blocks

Schoolhouse Block
Make 4.

Cutting

Cut all strips across the fabric width (selvage to selvage). Templates on pages 33 and 36.

From the red, cut:
1 strip, 6⅝" x 32"; crosscut into 24 pieces, each 1¼" x 6⅝", for A

1 strip, 3⅞" x 27"; crosscut into 16 pieces, each 1⅝" x 3⅞", for C
1 strip, 1⅝" x 42"; crosscut into 4 strips, each 1⅝" x 10", for E
4 Template F
4 Template H
1 strip, 1⅝" x 14"; crosscut into 8 squares, each 1⅝" x 1⅝", for J

From the cream, cut:
2 strips, each 2⅜" x 42"; crosscut into 12 pieces, each 2⅜" x 6⅝", for B
4 pieces, each 1⅝" x 3⅞", for C
1 strip, 3¼" x 32"; crosscut into 4 pieces, each 3¼" x 7¾", for D
2 strips, each 1⅝" x 42"; crosscut into 8 pieces, each 1⅝" x 10", for E
4 Template G
4 Template I
1 strip, 1⅝" x 14"; crosscut into 8 squares, each 1⅝" x 1⅝", for J
2 strips, each 2¾" x 42"; crosscut into 4 pieces, each 2¾" x 8⅜", for K
4 Template L

Piecing

1. Sew 3 A/B/A units.
2. Add piece C to the bottom of each A/B/A unit.

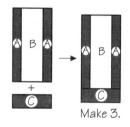

Make 3.

3. Sew one A/B/A/C unit to one side of piece D, and sew another A/B/A/C unit to the other side of piece D.

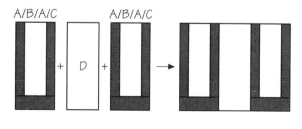

4. Sew 1 piece E of schoolhouse fabric to 1 piece E of background fabric. Sew this E/E unit to the top of A/B/A/C/D.

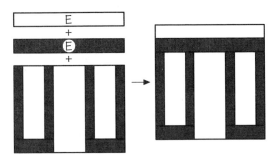

5. Sew 1 piece C of schoolhouse fabric to 1 piece C of background fabric. Sew this C/C unit to the remaining A/B/A/C unit.

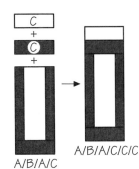

6. Sew piece E in between the 2 larger units made in steps 4 and 5.

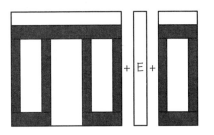

7. Sew piece F to piece G. Sew piece G to piece H.

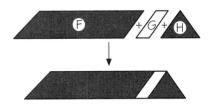

8. Sew 1 piece J of background fabric to 1 piece J of schoolhouse fabric. Repeat for the remaining J pieces.

Make 2.

9. Sew 1 pair J to each end of piece K.

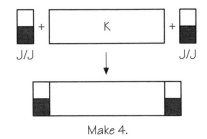

Make 4.

10. Sew the J/K unit to the F/G/H unit.

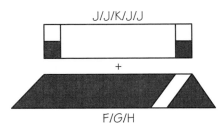

11. Sew piece I to the left side of J/K/F/G/H unit and sew piece L to the right side of the J/K/F/G/H unit.

12. Sew the completed schoolhouse top and bottom sections together. Make 4 Schoolhouse blocks.

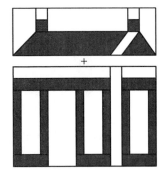

Lattice, Cornerstones, and Borders

Cutting

Cut all strips across the fabric width (selvage to selvage). Template on page 35.

From the green for lattice, cut:
6 strips, each 2½" x 42";
crosscut into 12 strips, each 2½" x 14½",
for lattice

From the plaid for cornerstones, cut:
1 strip, 2½" x 25"; crosscut into 9 squares,
each 2½" x 2½", for cornerstones

From the cream for borders, cut:
32 Template J
1 strip, 4⅜" x 42";
crosscut into 8 squares, each 4⅜" x 4⅜";
cut once diagonally for 16 triangles (N)
4 strips, each 1" x 42"

Piecing

1. Join Schoolhouse blocks into 2 horizontal rows with lattice strips as shown. Press all seams toward the lattice strips to eliminate bulk at seam intersections.

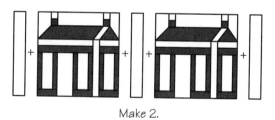

Make 2.

2. Make 3 rows of lattice and cornerstones as shown.

Make 3.

3. Join lattice/cornerstone rows to Schoolhouse rows as shown.

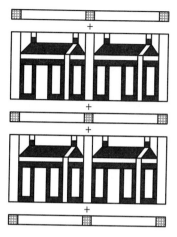

4. Sew the 1"-wide cream border strips to the quilt top, mitering corners as shown on pages 12–13.

Girl Blocks

Cutting

Cut all strips across the fabric width (selvage to selvage). Templates on pages 34–35.

From the cream, cut:
10 Template A for head
10 each Template C and Cr for arms
1 strip, 1¼" x 24"; crosscut into 20 pieces,
each 1⅛" x 1¼", for G (legs)

From the tan, cut:
10 Template J
20 Template D
1 strip, 1¼" x 13"; crosscut into 10 squares,
each 1¼" x 1¼", for F
10 squares, each 1⅝" x 1⅝";
cut once diagonally for 20 triangles (H)
10 Template I

From the blue plaid for the dress, cut:
10 each Template B and Br for sleeves
10 each Template E for dress

Piecing

Girls' Block Piecing Diagram (See page 34.)

1. Sew C to B and Cr to Br. Sew C/B unit to D, and Cr/Br unit to D.

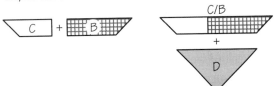

2. Sew C/B/D to E and Cr/Br/D to opposite side of E as shown.

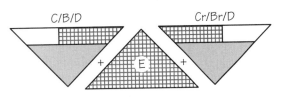

3. Sew a unit of H/G/F/G/H. Sew this unit to I.

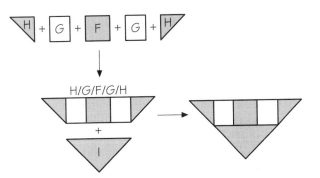

4. Join completed units together with piece J. Make 10 Girl blocks.

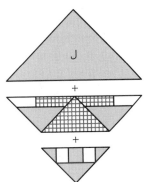

Boy Blocks

Cutting

Cut all strips across the fabric width (selvage to selvage). Templates on pages 34–35.

From the cream, cut:
10 Template A for head
10 each Template C and Cr for arms

From the tan, cut:
10 Template J
10 squares, each 2⅞" x 2⅞";
cut once diagonally for 20 triangles (L)
1 strip, 1¼" x 13"; crosscut into 10 squares,
each 1¼" x 1¼", for F
10 Template I

From the blue for the clothes, cut:
1 strip 1¼" x 12"; crosscut into 20 pieces,
each 1⅛" x 1¼", for G (pants)
1 strip, 2½" x 23"; crosscut into 10 pieces,
each 2¼" x 2½", for M (shirt)
1 strip, 1" x 31"; crosscut into 20 pieces,
each 1" x 1½", for K (sleeves)

Piecing

Boys' Block Piecing Diagram (See page 35.)

1. Sew C to K and Cr to K. Sew C/K unit to L, and Cr/K to L.

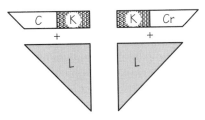

2. Sew a unit of G/F/G. Add piece I to the bottom of this unit, and piece M to the top of G/F/G unit.

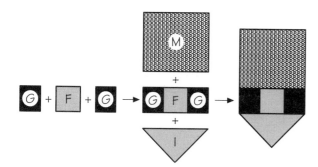

3. Sew a C/K/L unit to one side of I/G/F/G/M, and sew Cr/K/L unit to the other side of I/G/F/G/M.

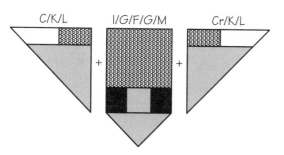

4. Join completed units together with piece J as shown. Make 10 Boy blocks.

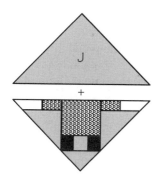

Appliqué and Embroidery

1. Following the directions on pages 10–11, cut and transfer markings for faces.
2. Appliqué the head onto the body of each Girl and Boy block.
3. Embroider the eyes with French knots, using 3 strands of floss. Embroider the mouth with a running stitch, using 2 strands of floss.
4. Sew lengths of embroidery floss around edge of head for hair and tie knots. Trim evenly.

Apple Blocks

Cutting

Templates on page 36.

From the tan, cut:
4 squares, each 7" x 7"

From the red, cut:
4 apples, using the apple template

From the red scraps, cut:
4 "windows" for apples

From the green scraps, cut:
4 leaves

Appliqué and Embroidery

Appliqué apples, windows on apples, and leaves to apple background square. With a stem stitch, embroider stem, vein in leaf, and detail on apple, using 2 strands of embroidery floss. Apple block piecing diagram is on page 36.

Kids Border Assembly

1. Make 4 kids' borders, alternating the Boy and Girl blocks. Use 5 blocks in each border, 8 triangles J, and 4 triangles N. Sew side borders to quilt top.
2. Sew an Apple block to each end of the top and bottom border strips. Sew borders to quilt top.

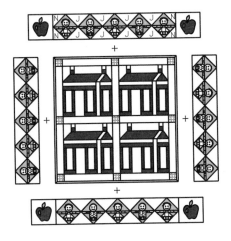

Finishing

Finish your quilt, following the quilt-finishing directions on pages 14–16.

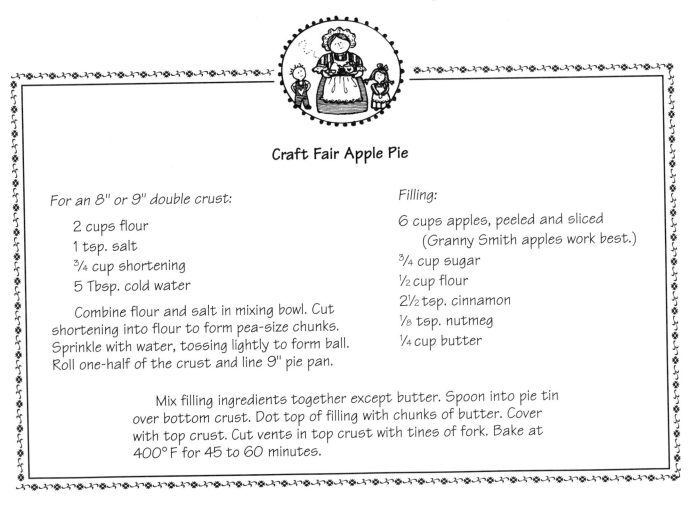

Craft Fair Apple Pie

For an 8" or 9" double crust:

2 cups flour
1 tsp. salt
3/4 cup shortening
5 Tbsp. cold water

Combine flour and salt in mixing bowl. Cut shortening into flour to form pea-size chunks. Sprinkle with water, tossing lightly to form ball. Roll one-half of the crust and line 9" pie pan.

Filling:

6 cups apples, peeled and sliced
(Granny Smith apples work best.)
3/4 cup sugar
1/2 cup flour
2 1/2 tsp. cinnamon
1/8 tsp. nutmeg
1/4 cup butter

Mix filling ingredients together except butter. Spoon into pie tin over bottom crust. Dot top of filling with chunks of butter. Cover with top crust. Cut vents in top crust with tines of fork. Bake at 400° F for 45 to 60 minutes.

Teach me Thy way O Lord; I will walk in Thy truth: unite my heart to fear Thy name. I will praise Thee, O Lord my God, with all my heart: and I will glorify Thy name for evermore. Psalm 86:11-12

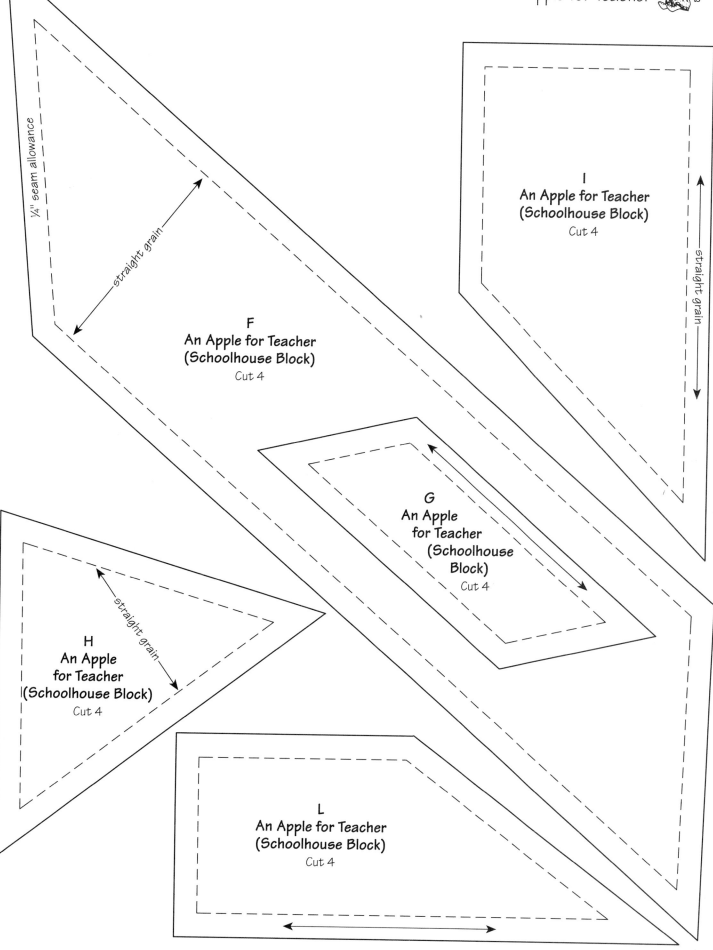

¼" seam allowance

straight grain

F
An Apple for Teacher
(Schoolhouse Block)
Cut 4

I
An Apple for Teacher
(Schoolhouse Block)
Cut 4

straight grain

G
An Apple
for Teacher
(Schoolhouse
Block)
Cut 4

H
An Apple
for Teacher
(Schoolhouse Block)
Cut 4

straight grain

L
An Apple for Teacher
(Schoolhouse Block)
Cut 4

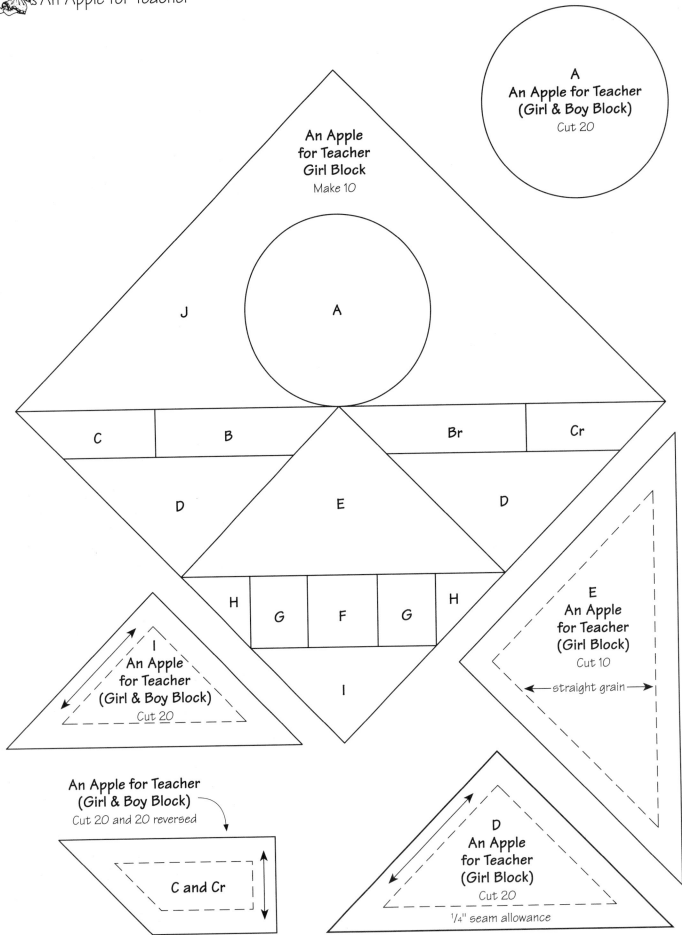

An Apple
for Teacher
Girl Block

Make 10

J

A

C   B   Br   Cr

D   E   D

H   G   F   G   H

I

A
An Apple for Teacher
(Girl & Boy Block)

Cut 20

I
An Apple
for Teacher
(Girl & Boy Block)

Cut 20

E
An Apple
for Teacher
(Girl Block)

Cut 10

straight grain

An Apple for Teacher
(Girl & Boy Block)

Cut 20 and 20 reversed

C and Cr

D
An Apple
for Teacher
(Girl Block)

Cut 20

1/4" seam allowance

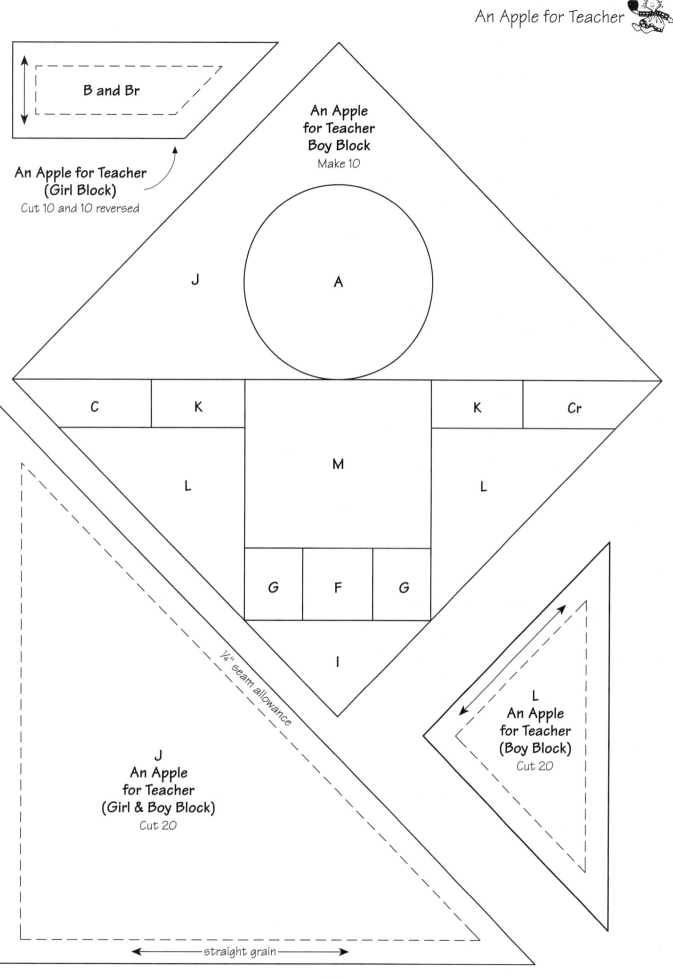

B and Br

An Apple for Teacher
(Girl Block)
Cut 10 and 10 reversed

An Apple
for Teacher
Boy Block
Make 10

J

A

C

K

K

Cr

M

L

L

G

F

G

I

¼" seam allowance

J
An Apple
for Teacher
(Girl & Boy Block)
Cut 20

L
An Apple
for Teacher
(Boy Block)
Cut 20

straight grain

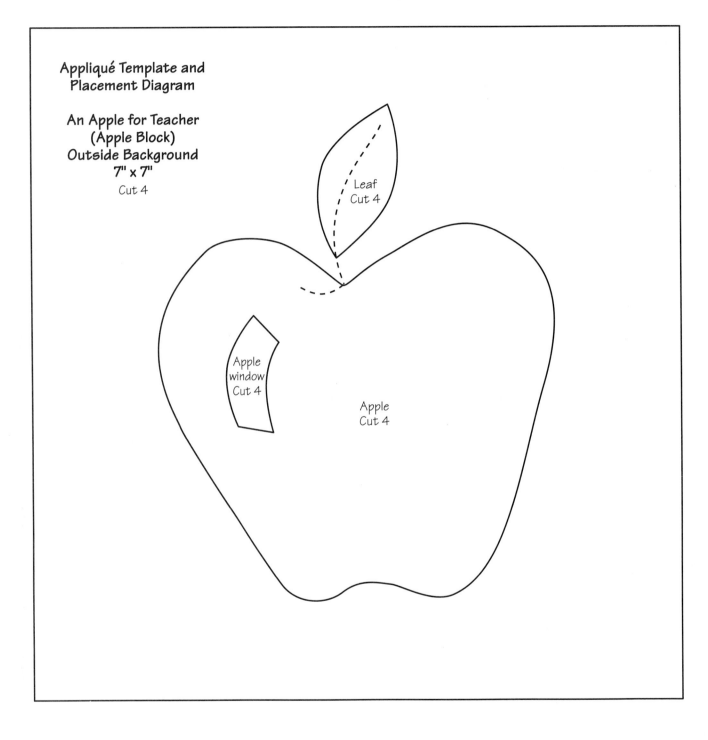

Appliqué Template and Placement Diagram

An Apple for Teacher (Apple Block) Outside Background 7" x 7" Cut 4

Leaf
Cut 4

Apple window
Cut 4

Apple
Cut 4

Gallery

Grandma's Garden Gate
Finished size: 38½" x 38½"

Friends gather to chat at this simply pieced gate. Appliquéd flowers trail around the trellis and along the fence line.

Mr. Grogan's Garden   Finished size: 29" x 36"

"Barry Grogan, how does your garden grow?" "With lollipops and
yo-yos all appliquéd in a row." Fantasy flowers embellished with
buttons and lace grow along a pieced fence and sky.

Little Sweethearts   Finished size: 6½"

Simple to construct, these ornaments may grace a country
Christmas tree, decorate a shelf, or hang on a wall all year-
round. Embellishing is the fun part—let your imagination
run wild!

Sweetheart Pocket   Finished size: 6" plus handle

Here's a beautifully decorated pocket made from old quilt pieces
(or new quilt pieces "aged" in a tea bath) and filled with goodies
of your choice.

Katie's Song
Finished size: 41¾" x 42½"

A randomly pieced background with appliquéd primitive figures tells the story of a little girl living in the forest with her animal friends. The simple appliqué work is embellished with embroidery, buttons, raffia, and charms.

An Apple for Teacher
Finished size: 49" x 49"

Happy children surround old-fashioned schoolhouses in a pieced wall quilt softened
with touches of appliqué and embroidery.

Can't See the Forest for the Christmas Trees
Finished size: 56" x 68"

Sparkling stars, a crescent moon, and a crisp mantle of snow magically transforms a forest
of evergreens into Christmas trees.

41

Hearts Aplenty Sampler
Finished size: 50" x 64" without lattice

The months and seasons of the year are the theme for this unusual pieced and appliquéd sampler made of woven checked and striped fabrics. Pictured are two versions of the quilt, one with lattice strips and one without.

Hearts Aplenty Sampler
Finished size: 60" x 76½" with lattice

Turkey in the Straw
Finished size: 41" x 41"

*A simple pieced block serves as the background for the appliquéd traditional messengers
announcing harvest time and Thanksgiving.*

Turkey in the Straw

Finished size: 41" x 41"   Quilt Plan

Fall harvest finds our favorite old Tom turkey, pumpkins, and hay sheaves on a simple pieced background for a cozy scene.

Color photo on page 44.

Materials: 44"-wide fabric

⅝ yd. green checked fabric for background fabric A

¾ yd. green for background fabric A and B

⅝ yd. cream for background fabric C

⅓ yd. each of 2 yellows for hay sheaves

¼ yd. each of 5 assorted oranges for pumpkins

⅛ yd. each of 3 assorted yellows for pumpkins

⅜ yd. rust for turkey's large back feathers

⅓ yd. blue for turkey's body

⅛ yd. each of assorted fabrics for turkey's neck, beak, feet, wattle, hearts, and bands around hay

Assorted scraps for pumpkin stems

¼ yd. orange for inner border

⅜ yd. green for outer border

⅔ yd. yellow for binding

1⅓ yds. for backing

48" x 48" piece of batting

Cutting for Pieced Background

Cut all strips across the fabric width (selvage to selvage).

From the green checked fabric, cut:
6 squares, each 9⅞" x 9⅞";
cut once diagonally for 12 triangles (A)

From the green, cut:
2 squares, each 9⅞" x 9⅞"; cut once
diagonally for 4 triangles (A)
2 squares, each 13⅝" x 13⅝"; cut once
diagonally for 4 triangles (B)

From the cream, cut:
1 square, 18½" x 18½"(C)

From the orange for the inner border, cut:
4 strips, each 1" x 42"

From the green for the outer border, cut:
4 strips, each 2½" x 42"

Directions

1. Sew A/A triangle pairs and A/B/A triangle sets together for Rows 1 and 3.

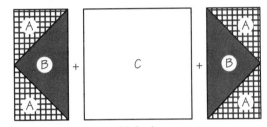

Make 2.

2. Sew A/B/A triangle sets to square C for Row 2.

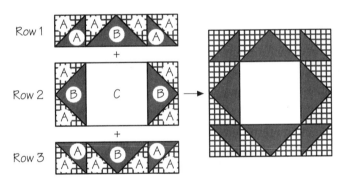

Make 1.

3. Sew Rows 1, 2, and 3 together as shown to complete the background.

Appliqué

Templates on pullout pattern insert.
Follow the instructions on pages 10–11 for cutting and sewing the appliqué pieces. The templates are numbered to help you with the sewing order. Layer the appliqué pieces from the background to the foreground.

Finishing

1. Measure the quilt for borders as shown on page 12. Sew to the quilt with mitered corners, following the directions on pages 12–13.
2. Finish your quilt, following the quilt-finishing directions on pages 14–16.

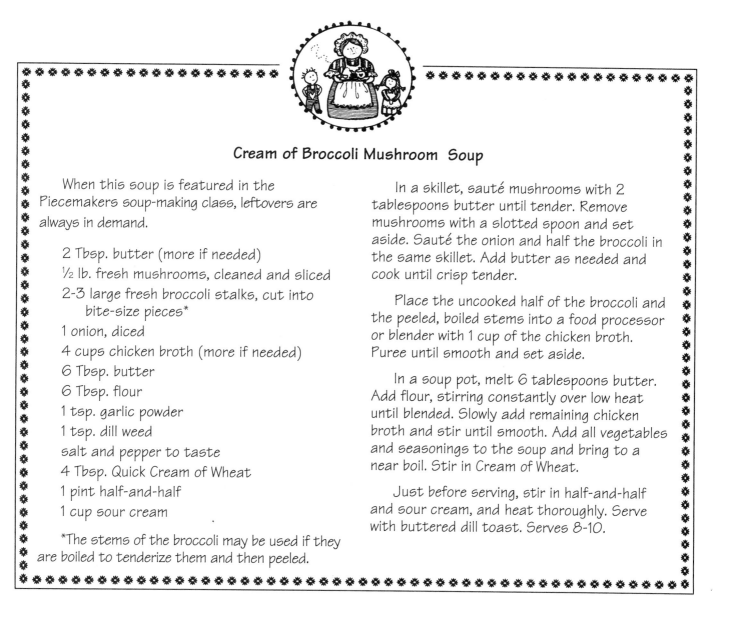

Cream of Broccoli Mushroom Soup

When this soup is featured in the Piecemakers soup-making class, leftovers are always in demand.

2 Tbsp. butter (more if needed)
½ lb. fresh mushrooms, cleaned and sliced
2-3 large fresh broccoli stalks, cut into bite-size pieces*
1 onion, diced
4 cups chicken broth (more if needed)
6 Tbsp. butter
6 Tbsp. flour
1 tsp. garlic powder
1 tsp. dill weed
salt and pepper to taste
4 Tbsp. Quick Cream of Wheat
1 pint half-and-half
1 cup sour cream

*The stems of the broccoli may be used if they are boiled to tenderize them and then peeled.

In a skillet, sauté mushrooms with 2 tablespoons butter until tender. Remove mushrooms with a slotted spoon and set aside. Sauté the onion and half the broccoli in the same skillet. Add butter as needed and cook until crisp tender.

Place the uncooked half of the broccoli and the peeled, boiled stems into a food processor or blender with 1 cup of the chicken broth. Puree until smooth and set aside.

In a soup pot, melt 6 tablespoons butter. Add flour, stirring constantly over low heat until blended. Slowly add remaining chicken broth and stir until smooth. Add all vegetables and seasonings to the soup and bring to a near boil. Stir in Cream of Wheat.

Just before serving, stir in half-and-half and sour cream, and heat thoroughly. Serve with buttered dill toast. Serves 8-10.

Make a joyful noise unto the Lord, all ye lands. Serve the Lord with gladness: come before His presence with singing. Know ye that the Lord He is God: it is He that hath made us, and not we ourselves; we are His people, and the sheep of His pasture. Enter into His gates with thanksgiving, and into His courts with praise: be thankful unto Him, and bless His name. For the Lord is good; His mercy is everlasting; and His truth endureth to all generations. Psalm 100

Hearts Aplenty Sampler

Finished size: 50" x 64"   Appliqué Diagrams

Twelve charming scenes, one for each month of the year, are framed by simple pieced blocks, making this an appealing quilt for anyone. Look for the heart in each block!

Color photo on page 42.

Materials: 44"-wide fabric

1½ yds. light-background print or solid for Templates A, D, and Dr

⅞ yd. dark print for Template B and Br

¾ yd. dark print for Template C and Cr

⅝ yd. medium print or plaid for Template E

Assorted medium prints, plaids, or solids of 3 to 5 fabrics to total ⅔ yd. for F (minimum width 4")

¼ yd. each (or scraps) of 12 to 18 assorted fabrics for appliqué

1 yd. checked fabric for border

3½ yds. for backing quilt without lattice*

1 yd. for binding

56" x 70" piece of batting

Embroidery floss in black, brown, red, green, and blue

1 button or small buckle

3" piece of ½"-wide lace for February block

**See page 51 for additional materials
to make quilt with lattice.*

Cutting for Pieced Blocks

Cut all strips across the fabric width (selvage to selvage). Templates on page 52.

From the light-background print or solid, cut:
3 strips, each 7½" x 42"; crosscut into 12 squares, each 7½" x 7½", for A
Cut 48 Template D and 48 Template Dr

From the first dark print, cut:
48 Template B and 48 Template Br

From the second dark print, cut:
48 Template C and 48 Template Cr

From the medium print or plaid, cut:
48 Template E

From assorted medium fabrics, cut:
5 strips, each 4" x 42"; crosscut into 48 squares, each 4" x 4", for F

From the checked fabric for border, cut:
7 strips, each 4½" x 42"

Directions

Pieced Blocks

The directions that follow are for the sampler quilt *without* lattice and cornerstones. Directions for lattice and cornerstones appear on page 51. Make 12 blocks, following the directions below.

1. Sew piece C to piece D. Sew piece Cr to piece Dr. Sew C/D units to Cr/Dr units, ending stitching at the ¼" seam intersection on the inside point.

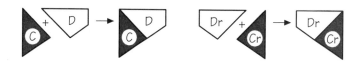

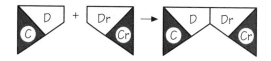

End stitching here.

2. Sew piece B to one side of E and piece Br to the other side of E.

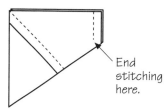

3. Sew the B/E/Br unit to the C/D/Dr/Cr unit, stitching from the center point in the directions of the arrows.

Make 48 units.

4. Add a piece F to each end of the B/C/D/E unit.

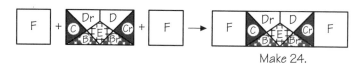

Make 24.

5. Sew a B/C/D/E unit to one side of piece A. Sew another B/C/D/E unit to the opposite side of the same piece A.

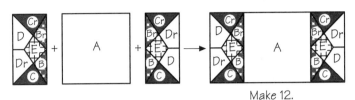

Make 12.

6. Sew the 3 units together for a 14" block.

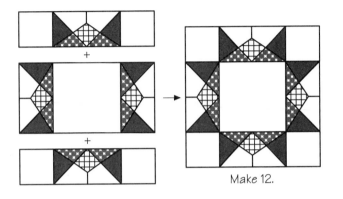

Make 12.

Appliqué

Templates on pullout pattern insert.

Follow the directions on page 10 for tracing and cutting the appliqué pieces. Some of the appliqué pieces overlap each other, so appliqué in order from the background to the foreground. The appliqué templates are numbered to help you with the sewing order. Add appliqués to the completed quilt blocks and embroider as many of the details as possible *before* sewing all the blocks together.

Embroidery

Refer to page 9 for general embroidery instructions. Use three strands of floss to embroider French knots for eyes. Use two strands of floss to embroider a stem stitch for snowman's mouth and arms, bunny's nose, lines on seashell, book spines, and the leaves and vines on the pumpkin. Sew a button or buckle on the book strap.

Quilt Top Assembly and Finishing

1. Sew the blocks together in order by months, with 3 blocks across by 4 blocks down.

Jan.	Feb.	Mar.
+		
April	May	June
+		
July	Aug.	Sept.
+		
Oct.	Nov.	Dec.

2. Join the border strips into one long piece.
3. Measure the quilt for borders as shown on page 12, and attach to quilt with your choice of straight-cut or mitered corners.
4. Finish your quilt, following the quilt-finishing directions on pages 14–16.

Optional Lattice

Finished size of quilt with lattice: 60" x 76½"

Color photo on page 43.

Materials: 44"-wide fabric

1⅜ yds. for lattice strips

1¼ yds. for border

3" cornerstones of 1 color (¼ yd.) or assorted appliqué fabric scraps

4 yds. for backing

66" x 83" piece of batting

Cutting

Cut all strips across the fabric width (selvage to selvage).

From the lattice fabric, cut:
31 lattice strips, each 3" x 14½"

From the cornerstone fabric, cut:
20 squares, each 3" x 3", for cornerstones

From the border fabric, cut:
8 strips, each 4½" x 42"

Quilt Top Assembly and Finishing

1. Sew the cornerstones to the horizontal lattice strips as shown. Sew the vertical lattice strips to the block sides. Assemble the lattice and the quilt blocks as shown.
2. Measure the quilt for borders as shown on pages 12–13, and attach to the quilt with your choice of straight-cut or mitered corners.
3. Finish your quilt, following the quilt-finishing directions on pages 14–16.

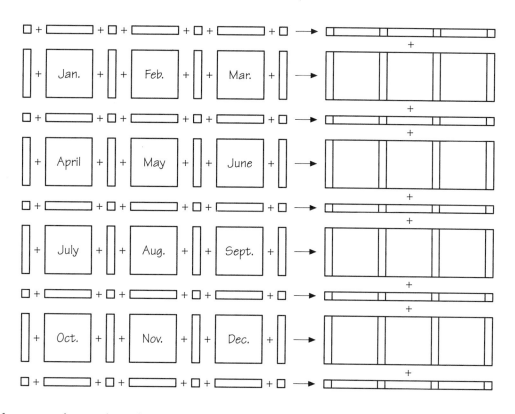

So teach us to number our days, that we may apply our hearts to wisdom. O satisfy us early with Thy mercy; that we may rejoice and be glad all our days. Let the beauty of the Lord our God be upon us; and establish Thou the work of our hands; yea, the work of our hands establish Thou it. Psalm 90:12, 15, and 17

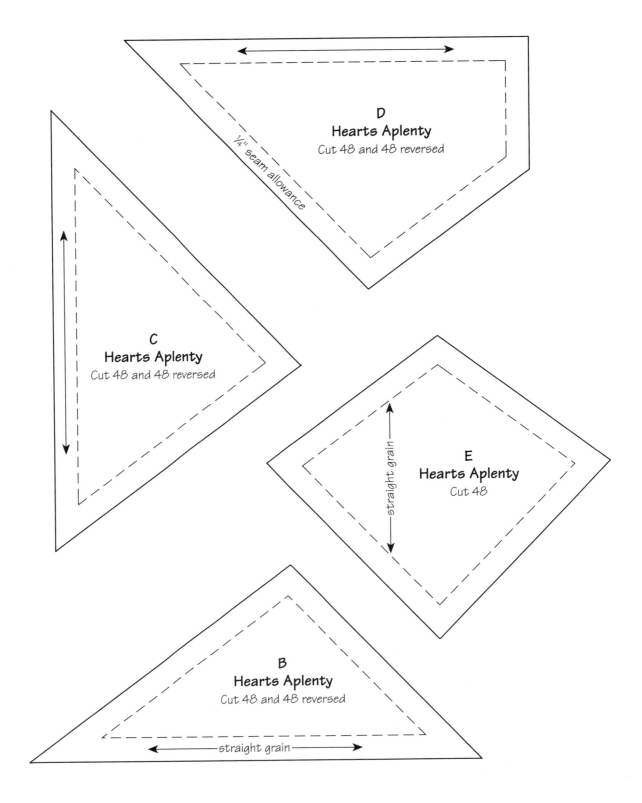

D
Hearts Aplenty
Cut 48 and 48 reversed

¼" seam allowance

C
Hearts Aplenty
Cut 48 and 48 reversed

E
Hearts Aplenty
Cut 48

straight grain

B
Hearts Aplenty
Cut 48 and 48 reversed

straight grain

Katie's Song

Finished size: 41¾" x 42½"   Quilt Plan

This wall hanging was inspired by a story one of the Piecemakers wrote for another Piecemaker.

If you look carefully to the east, west, north, and south in the quilt, you'll meet all of Katie's friends mentioned in the story, surrounding her with music in the woods.

This quilt was embellished with old buttons, embroidery, and lots of dangling treats. This is a form of crazy quilting—only ours is primitive on purpose. Embroidery stitches are large and little treasures are hidden everywhere to give the viewers endless enjoyment.

Katie's Song

There once was a girl who lived in a small house in the country, very far away from the city. Although she had no neighbors, she was never lonely. This was because she loved walking throughout the land and seeing all the animals that lived in her neighborhood. There were families of cute little cuddly critters, herds of fast-running, long-legged beasts, and schools of shining, darting fish. Her favorite animals, by far, were the ones that could fly in the beautiful blue country skies. These, she knew, were somehow special.

One day, as she was walking in the warm sunshine near the edge of a canyon to the north of her house, she spied a lone eagle soaring gracefully in the clouds. Suddenly, the eagle dived straight down towards her. She was frozen stiff with fear and could not move. At the very last moment, the eagle pulled up from the dive and spread its wings across the sun so that the shadow of its wings covered the girl. It might have been her imagination, but she thought she heard the eagle say:

Glory, glory, glory to the
Lord God Almighty
Patient in love and a terror
to see.
When you fear death or
ugly things
Find shelter in the shadow
of my wings.

Almost as soon as it happened, the eagle flapped its wings and sped off, back to the high places. Katie was startled, but soon recovered, and was walking again and feeling the warm sunshine. She didn't think too much again about the eagle and what had happened.

The next day, as she was walking in the cool of the morning in the woods to the south of her house, Katie heard a noise. She stopped and quickly hid behind a tree. At first, all she heard was the pounding of her own heart, but soon she heard another noise and then another, and then what sounded like a chorus of singing. She peered around the tree and saw a flock of turtledoves, singing what was almost a lullaby. It might have been her imagination, but she thought she heard this song:

Turtle Lee, Turtle Lie,
Into the Lord's comfort draw nigh.
Turtle Lee, Turtle Loo,
Oh, how much I love you!

Just then, the birds scampered away into the air, squawking gibberish. This time, she pondered in her heart what this might mean and returned home.

The next day, Katie went walking down by the pond to the east of her home. She sat down among the reeds on the shore and watched several hundred snow geese as they circled around in an unhurried flight above the water. They stayed in perfect order, each in its own place, until they all landed in the water. It might have been her imagination or maybe the wind in the reeds, but Katie thought she heard the geese saying:

Honk, Honk. I know my place;
I follow the leader at his pace.
Honk, Honk. We travel as one;
As unity with our Lord is done.

Just then, they all lifted up together and flew away toward the warm southern breezes. Again, she pondered in her heart what this might mean and returned home.

The next day, Katie was still thinking about the eagle's shadow, the turtledove's love, and the geese's unity as she was walking in the barren rock fields to the west of her house. Out of the corner of her eye, she saw a flitter and a flutter from behind a rock. As she slowly walked around to the back of the rock, she began to distinguish a sound. It was something like a buzzing, but soon became more like a clapping and then suddenly sounded like an audience requesting an encore. The sound grew to a roar as thousands of butterflies burst from the rock, flapping their beautiful purple and crimson wings and swirling upward in flight. This time, she knew it was not her imagination but the butterflies beating their wings to this song:

Praise and Thanks, we give dear Lord to Thee;
No longer worms, but truly free.
Praise and Thanks in our flight;
You changed us with Your blessed might.

In a blink of an eye, the butterflies were gone, but this time the song remained in her heart forever.

Color photo on page 39.

Materials: 44"-wide fabric

⅛ yd. each (or scraps) of assorted fabrics for songbirds, music notes, rabbits, fish, fronds around the pond, butterflies, chimney, gable, window, door, tree trunks, caterpillar, girl, girl's dress, apron, and heart

¼ yd. each (or scraps) of assorted fabrics for snow geese, house roof, trees, pond, eagle, and mountains

⅜ yd. yellow for the sun

¼ yd. each of 7 fabrics* for backgrounds A, C, F, G, H, I, and J (Choose an assortment of stripes, checks, and plaids for the homespun look.)

⅓ yd. each of 2 fabrics* for backgrounds B and E

½ yd. for background D, behind girl

⅝ yd. for border

1⅓ yds. for backing

⅔ yd. for binding

46" x 46" piece of batting

Embroidery floss for hair, eyes, mouth, music-note stems, sun, and to embellish the appliqués as desired

Old buttons, charms, raffia, and other treasures you wish to use for embellishment

*You may want to repeat some of these background fabrics instead of using all different ones.

Cutting for Pieced Top

Cut all strips across the fabric width (selvage to selvage).

Cut out background and border pieces as listed below. All measurements include ¼"-wide seam allowances.

1 piece A - 5¾" x 35¼"
1 piece B - 9½" x 20¾"
1 piece C - 6" x 26¼"
1 piece D - 13" x 17½"
1 piece E - 9¼" x 13"
1 piece F - 5" x 10½"
1 piece G - 5" x 10½"
1 piece H - 5¾" x 26¼"
1 piece I - 7½" x 13½"
1 piece J - 7½" x 13¼"
Border: 2 strips, each 4" x 35¼",
and 2 strips, each 4" x 43"*

* You may need to piece the border strips if your fabric is not at least 43" wide.

Directions

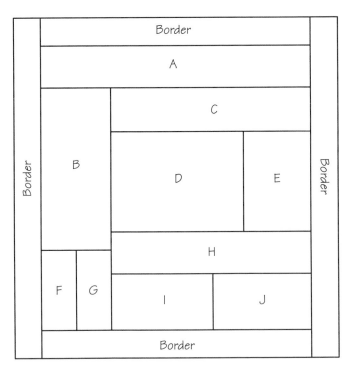

Using ¼"-wide seam allowances, piece the background in the following sequence.

1. Sew F to G and then to B as shown, making Unit B/F/G. Set aside.

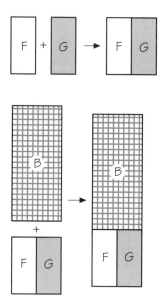

2. Sew D to E and then to C, making Unit C/D/E. Set aside.

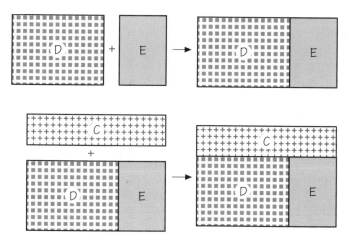

3. Sew I to J and then to H, making Unit H/I/J. Set aside.

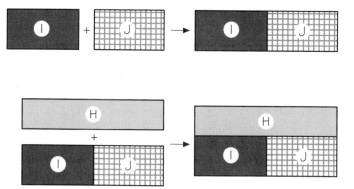

4. Sew Unit C/D/E to Unit H/I/J.

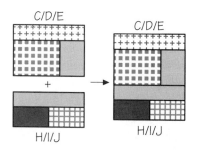

5. Sew Unit B/F/G to Unit C/D/E/H/I/J.

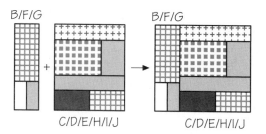

6. Sew A to the unit completed in step 5.

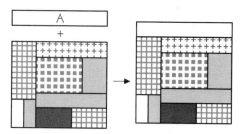

7. Sew the top and bottom border strips to the quilt top, then add the side borders.

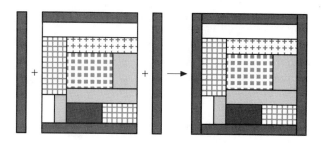

Appliqué

Dotted lines on template pieces indicate where appliqués overlap. Most of the pieces do not overlap each other, so you can appliqué them in any order you like. Placement of the appliqué pieces may vary a little on this wall hanging since it is a picture you are creating.

Refer to page 10 for general directions on tracing and cutting the appliqué pattern pieces. Add ¼"-wide seam allowances around appliqués as you cut them from the selected fabrics. Appliqué pieces to quilt top, using a Piecemakers hand appliqué needle for tiny, smooth stitches. Refer to quilt plan on page 53 for appliqué placement. Appliqué patterns are on pullout pattern insert.

Finishing

1. Add the finishing touches with embroidery. Refer to the quilt photo on page 39 and the general directions on page 9 for specific stitches. Using the stem stitch, embroider the doves' legs, the caterpillar's antennae, the butterflies' antennae, the log lines on the house, and the stems on the music notes. Using 3 strands of embroidery floss, embroider the eyes with French knots. Using 2 strands of floss, embroider the girl's mouth and around the sun with a running stitch.

2. Make the girl's hair by tying lengths of 3 strands of embroidery floss as shown. After tying the knots, trim ends of floss evenly.

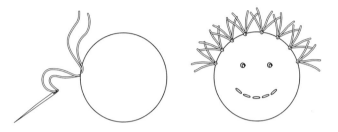

3. Add old buttons, charms, stones, and raffia bows to embellish and to give a three-dimensional effect. Add these special touches to your heart's delight. Work extra embroidery wherever you want more dimension. A running stitch done with raffia gives an interesting effect. You'll need a needle grabber to pull the needle through the layers.

4. Finish your wall hanging, following the quilt-finishing directions on pages 14–16.

For the Lord shall comfort Zion: He will comfort all her waste places;
and He will make her wilderness like Eden, and her desert like the garden of the Lord;
joy and gladness shall be found therein, thanksgiving, and the voice of melody. Isaiah 51:3

Sing for Me!

What's that I hear
That awakens My soul?
A voice out of heaven
That catches My ear.
Like the voice of the turtle,
Do you hear, do you see?
Oh Katie, step forward and sing for Me.

I buried that music deep in your earth,
Knowing one day you'd labor and birth
Sweet psalms and sweet music
For the whole world to see—
Come Katie, come forward and sing for Me.

I've walked with you, Katie,
Through your pain and sorrow.
I heard that sweet music
That would come on the morrow.
With patience and tears you walked close,
now see—
Come Katie, come forward and sing for Me.

You gave Me your heart,
I gave you My hand,
You gave up the world,
Now I am your Man
Who has formed you and shaped you,
My delight—all to see
Oh Katie—I love you—please sing for Me.

Oh sing on, little Katie,
For the springtime is here,
The soul-searching music
Will hearken the ear
Of man and of beast, of bird and of bee,
Come Katie, come forward and sing for Me!

1984

Can't See the Forest for the Christmas Trees

Finished size: 56" x 68"   Quilt Plan

Christmas reds, greens, blues, and golds proclaim the magic of the season. The stars sparkle amid the snow-covered evergreens.

Color photo on page 41.

Materials: 44"-wide fabric

½ yd. white for centers of Star Block A and snow

Scraps of yellow for crescent moon and star

⅜ yd. each of 2 fabrics (yellow or gold) for Star Block B

⅝ yd. each of 2 blues (dark and medium dark) for pieces A and C of Star blocks

½ yd. each of 3 tans for background fabrics

⅛ yd. each of 2 browns for tree trunks

⅛ yd. each of 3 reds for hearts

⅜ yd. each of 6 assorted light, medium, and dark greens for trees

⅝ yd. each of red, green, and brown for setting strips

½ yd. red for inner border

1 yd. green for outer border

3½ yds. for backing

¾ yd. for binding

62" x 74" piece of batting

Black DMC Perle Cotton #5 or #8

Star Blocks

Make 5 of the first color variation and 5 of the second variation.

Cutting

Cut all strips across the fabric width (selvage to selvage). All measurements include ¼"-wide seam allowances.

Variation 1

From the medium dark blue, cut:
2 strips, each 3½" x 42"; crosscut into
20 squares, each 3½" x 3½", for Piece A
2 strips, each 3⅞" x 42"
Trace 20 Template C onto strips and cut.

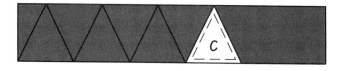

From the white, cut:
1 strip, 3½" x 42"; crosscut into 5 squares,
each 3½" x 3½", for Piece A. Set leftover strip aside.

From the yellow, cut:
20 Template B and 20 Template B reversed

From the reds for hearts, cut:
5 small hearts, using the appliqué
pattern on pullout pattern insert.

Variation 2

From the dark blue, cut:
2 strips, each 3½" x 42"; crosscut into 20 squares,
each 3½" x 3½", for Piece A
2 strips, each 3⅞" x 42"
Trace 20 Template C onto strips and
cut as shown for Variation 1.

From the remaining white strip for star centers, cut:
5 squares, each 3½" x 3½", for Piece A

From the gold, cut:
20 Template B and 20 Template B reversed

From the reds for hearts, cut:
5 small hearts, using the appliqué
pattern on pullout pattern insert.

Piecing

Follow the general directions for piecing on page 10 and the appliqué directions on pages 10–11 to assemble the blocks.

Make 5 of Variation 1
and 5 of Variation 2.

Star Block

1. Sew 1 B and 1 Br to 1 C. Make 4 units for each Star block.

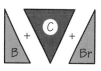

2. Appliqué a heart to center square for each block.
3. Sew the units together in rows as shown.
4. Join the rows to complete the Star block.

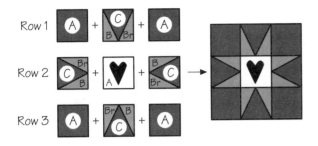

Tree Blocks

There are 12 different Tree blocks. Tree Blocks 1, 2, 7, and 12 are appliqué blocks. Follow the directions for using appliqué patterns on pages 10–11 and refer to the quilt photo on page 41. Appliqué pieces in place as shown in the block diagrams. Appliqué patterns are on the pullout pattern insert.

Tree Blocks 3, 4, 5, 6, 8, 9, 10, and 11 are pieced blocks. Except for the appliqué pieces, measurements include ¼"-wide seam allowances. Template patterns are on pages 71–74.

Tree Block #1

Tree Block #1
Appliqué Placement

1. Cut 1 rectangle, 6½" x 9½", from background fabric.
2. Using templates for Tree Block 1, cut the tree top, middle, bottom, and tree trunk.
3. Appliqué pieces in place on the block background. Appliqué pieces are numbered in the block diagram in the order they are to be sewn.

Tree Block #2

Tree Block #2
Appliqué Placement

1. Cut 1 rectangle, 9½" x 15½", from background fabric.
2. Using the appliqué pattern pieces, cut the large, medium, and small trees and trunks; medium star; and snow.
3. Appliqué pieces are numbered in the block diagram in the order they are to be sewn.

Tree Block #7

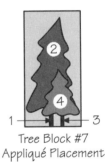

Tree Block #7
Appliqué Placement

1. Cut 1 rectangle, 6½" x 12½", from background fabric.
2. Using the appliqué patterns on the pullout pattern insert, cut 1 tall tree, 1 short tree, and tree trunks.
3. Appliqué pieces are numbered in the block diagram in the order they are to be sewn.

Tree Block #12

Tree Block #12
Appliqué Placement

1. Cut 1 rectangle, 6½" x 9½", from background fabric.
2. Using the appliqué patterns, cut 1 each of left and right trees, snow, and small star.
3. Appliqué pieces are numbered in the block diagram in the order they are to be sewn.

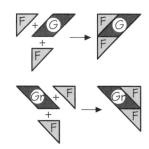

Tree Block #3

Tree Block #3

Appliqué heart last.

Cutting

From the background fabric, cut:
1 square, 6⅞" x 6⅞"; cut once diagonally
to yield 2 triangles (D)
2 squares, each 3⅞" x 3⅞"; cut once diagonally
to yield 4 triangles (F)
2 rectangles, each 6" x 3½", for Piece I

From the dark greens, cut:
2 Template E

From the medium greens, cut:
1 square, 3⅞" x 3⅞"; cut once
diagonally to yield 2 triangles (F)
1 Template G and 1 Template G reversed

From the light greens, cut:
1 Template H - cut on fold

From the tree trunk fabrics, cut:
1 rectangle, 1½" x 3½", for Piece J

From the reds for hearts, cut:
1 large heart

Piecing

1. Sew 2 D/E/F units.

Make 2.

2. Sew units together as shown.

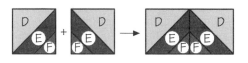

3. Sew F/G/F unit and F/Gr/F unit.

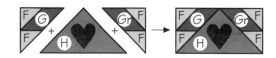

4. Sew the F/G/F and F/Gr/F units to H.

5. Sew I/J/I unit.

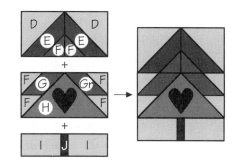

6. Appliqué the large heart to piece H.
7. Join the rows to complete the block.

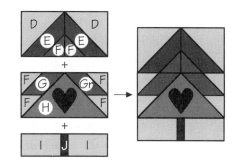

Tree Block #4

Cutting

From the background fabric, cut:
3 squares, each 3⅞" x 3⅞"; cut once diagonally
to yield 6 triangles (F)
2 rectangles, each 3⅛" x 3½", for L

From each of the 6 tree fabrics, cut:
1 strip, 1¼" x 42"; sew strips together lengthwise
with ¼"-wide seam allowances
Cut 3 Template K from the strip-pieced unit.

Use Template K to cut
3 triangles.

From tree trunk fabrics, cut:
1 rectangle, 1¼" x 3½", for Piece M

Piecing

1. Sew 3 F/K/F units, alternating the direction of the strips as shown.

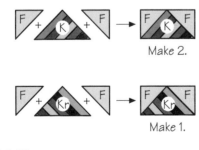

2. Sew L/M/L.

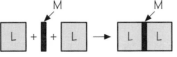

3. Join rows to complete block.

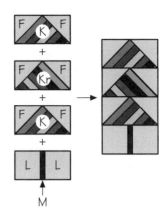

Tree Blocks #5 and #9

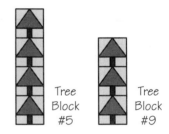

Cutting

Make 4 trees for Tree Block 5, and 3 trees for

From the background fabric, cut:
7 Template N and 7 Template N reversed
14 rectangles, each 1¾" x 1½", for Piece P

From the tree fabrics, cut:
7 Template O

From the tree trunk fabrics, cut:
7 rectangles, each 1" x 1½", for Piece Q

Piecing

1. Sew 7 N/O/Nr units.

2. Sew 7 P/Q/P units.

Make 7.

3. Join the N/O/Nr units to the P/Q/P units. Make 7.

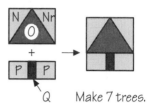

Make 7 trees.

4. Join 4 trees for Block 5 and 3 trees for Block 9.

Block #5   Block #9

Tree Block #6

Tree Block #6

Cutting

From the background fabric, cut:
1 Template S and 1 Template S reversed
1 square, 6⅞" x 6⅞"; cut once diagonally
to yield 2 triangles (D)
2 rectangles, each 3½" x 6⅛", for Piece I

From the tree fabrics, cut:
1 Template R
1 Template T

From the tree trunk fabrics, cut:
1 rectangle, 3½" x 1¼", for Piece J

From the scraps of yellow, cut:
1 crescent moon and 1 large star

Piecing

1. Appliqué the crescent moon onto background Piece S.
2. Sew unit S/R/Sr.

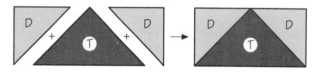

3. Sew D/T/D.

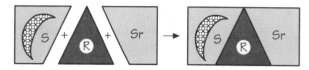

4. Sew unit I/J/I.

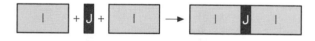

5. Join the units to complete the block.
6. Appliqué the star in place.

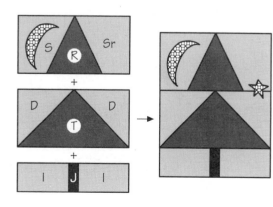

Tree Block #8

Tree Block #8

Cutting

From the background fabric, cut:
2 squares, each 3⅛" x 3⅛"; cut once diagonally
to yield 4 triangles Y
2 Template U and 2 Template U reversed

From the 5 different tree fabrics, cut:
2 each Template W
2 each Template X

From the tree trunk fabrics, cut:
2 Template V

Piecing

1. Sew 2 U/V/Ur units.

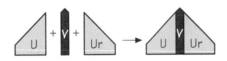

2. Beginning with W, alternate sewing the W and X pieces to the U/V/Ur units until all the pieces are added.

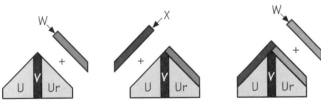

3. Sew 1 Y piece to the top of each side of the trees to complete the blocks.

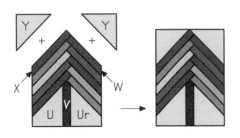

Tree Block #10

Tree Block #10

Cutting

From the background fabric, cut:
2 squares, each 3⅞" x 3⅞"; cut once diagonally
to yield 4 triangles (F)
2 rectangles, each 3¼" x 3½", for Piece AA

From the dark tree fabric, cut:
3 squares, each 3" x 3"; cut once diagonally
to yield 6 triangles (Z)

From the medium tree fabric, cut:
1 square, 3" x 3"; cut once diagonally
to yield 2 triangles (Z)

From the tree trunk fabrics, cut:
1 rectangle, 1" x 3½", for Piece BB

Piecing

1. Sew 2 Z/Z/Z/Z units as shown.

2. Sew 1 triangle F to each side of the Z units.

3. Sew AA/BB/AA.

4. Join the units to complete the block.

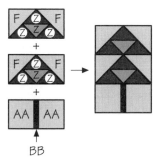

Tree Block #11

Tree Block #11

Cutting

From the background fabric, cut:
1 square, 3⅞" x 3⅞"; cut once diagonally
to yield 2 triangles (F)
1 Template CC and 1 Template CC reversed

From the 6 different tree fabrics, cut:
1 each Template EE
1 each Template FF

From the tree trunk fabrics, cut:
1 Template DD

Piecing
Blocks

1. Sew CC/DD/CCr unit.

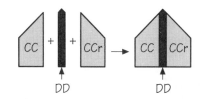

2. Beginning with EE, alternate sewing Pieces EE and FF to the CC/DD/CCr unit until all the pieces are added as for Tree Block 8.

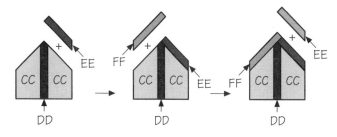

3. Sew 1 Piece F to each side of the tree to complete the block.

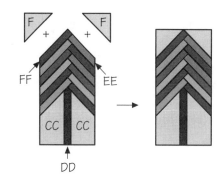

Setting Strips

*Cut all strips across the fabric
width (selvage to selvage).*

1. Cut 11 strips, each 1½" x 42", from brown, red,
   and green fabrics.
2. Sew 11 sets of 3 strips as shown for setting the blocks.

— Brown
— Red
— Green

3. Cut strip sets into the following lengths:

1 strip	6½"	Tree Block 7
13 strips	9½"	Tree Blocks 1, 2, 8, 12; 6 Star blocks
5 strips	12½"	Tree Blocks 3, 4, 11
1 strip	15½"	Tree Block 7
2 strips	18½"	Tree Block 5, Middle Section
2 strips	21½"	Tree Block 5, Bottom Section
1 strip	24½"	Bottom Section
1 strip	27½"	Middle Section
1 strip	33½"	Bottom Section

Variation 2
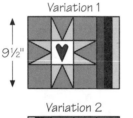
12½"
9½"

Tree Block #12
9½"

Tree Block #1
9½"

Tree Block #8
9½"

Tree Block #4
12½"

Tree Block #2
9½"

Tree Block #5
18½"
21½"

Tree Block #11
12½"

Tree Block #7
6½"
15½"

Tree Block #3
12½"

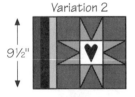
Variation 2
9½"

Variation 1
9½"

Variation 1
9½"

Variation 2
9½"

Variation 2
9½"

Variation 1
9½"

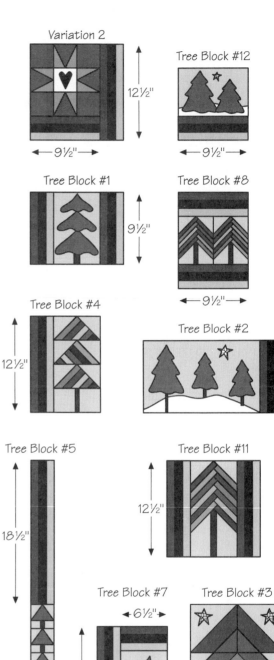

4. Assemble the top section as shown.

Top section

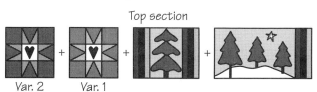

Var. 2   Var. 1

5. Assemble the middle section as shown.

Middle section

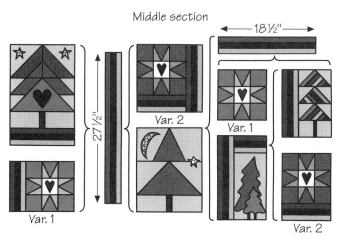

Var. 1

Var. 2   Var. 1

Var. 2

18½"

27½"

6. Assemble the bottom section as shown.

Bottom section

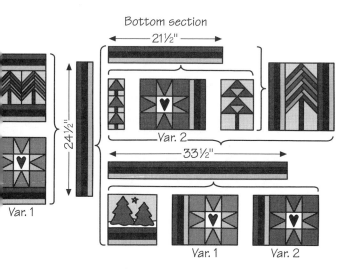

Var. 1

21½"

24½"

Var. 2

33½"

Var. 1   Var. 2

7. Join the middle and bottom sections, and add Tree Block #5 section to the left side. Add the top section to complete the quilt top.

Finishing

1. Cut 8 strips, each 1½" x 42", from inner border fabric.
2. Cut 8 strips, each 3½" x 42", from outer border fabric.
3. Measure the quilt for mitered borders and attach as shown on pages 12–13.
4. Finish your quilt, following the quilt-finishing directions on pages 14–16.

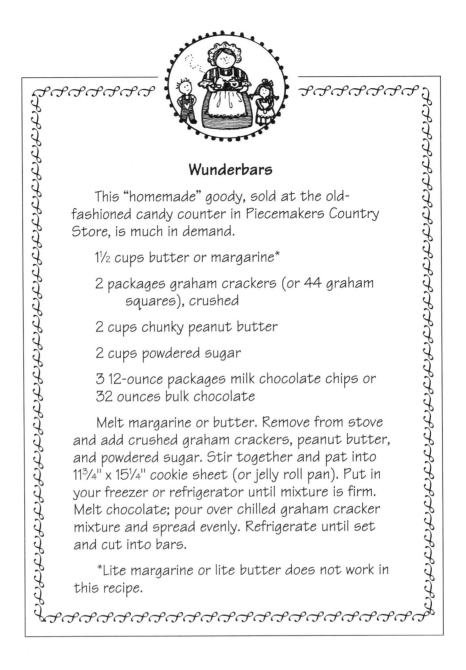

Wunderbars

This "homemade" goody, sold at the old-fashioned candy counter in Piecemakers Country Store, is much in demand.

1½ cups butter or margarine*

2 packages graham crackers (or 44 graham squares), crushed

2 cups chunky peanut butter

2 cups powdered sugar

3 12-ounce packages milk chocolate chips or 32 ounces bulk chocolate

Melt margarine or butter. Remove from stove and add crushed graham crackers, peanut butter, and powdered sugar. Stir together and pat into 11¾" x 15¼" cookie sheet (or jelly roll pan). Put in your freezer or refrigerator until mixture is firm. Melt chocolate; pour over chilled graham cracker mixture and spread evenly. Refrigerate until set and cut into bars.

*Lite margarine or lite butter does not work in this recipe.

*And Jesus cometh to Bethsaida; and they bring a blind man unto Him,
and besought Him to touch him.
And He took the blind man by the hand, and led him out of the town; and when
He had spit on his eyes, and put His hands upon him,
He asked him if he saw ought.
And he looked up, and said, I see men as trees, walking.
After that, Jesus put His hands again upon his eyes, and made him look up:
and he was restored, and saw every man clearly. Mark 8: 22-25*

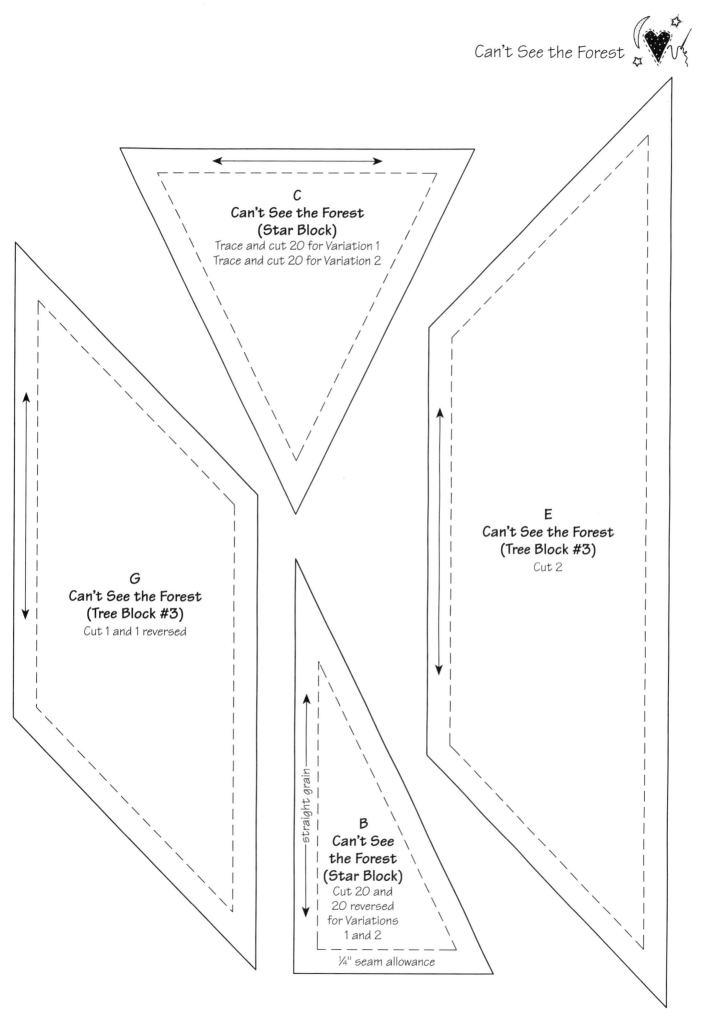

C
Can't See the Forest
(Star Block)
Trace and cut 20 for Variation 1
Trace and cut 20 for Variation 2

E
Can't See the Forest
(Tree Block #3)
Cut 2

G
Can't See the Forest
(Tree Block #3)
Cut 1 and 1 reversed

straight grain

B
Can't See
the Forest
(Star Block)
Cut 20 and
20 reversed
for Variations
1 and 2

¼" seam allowance

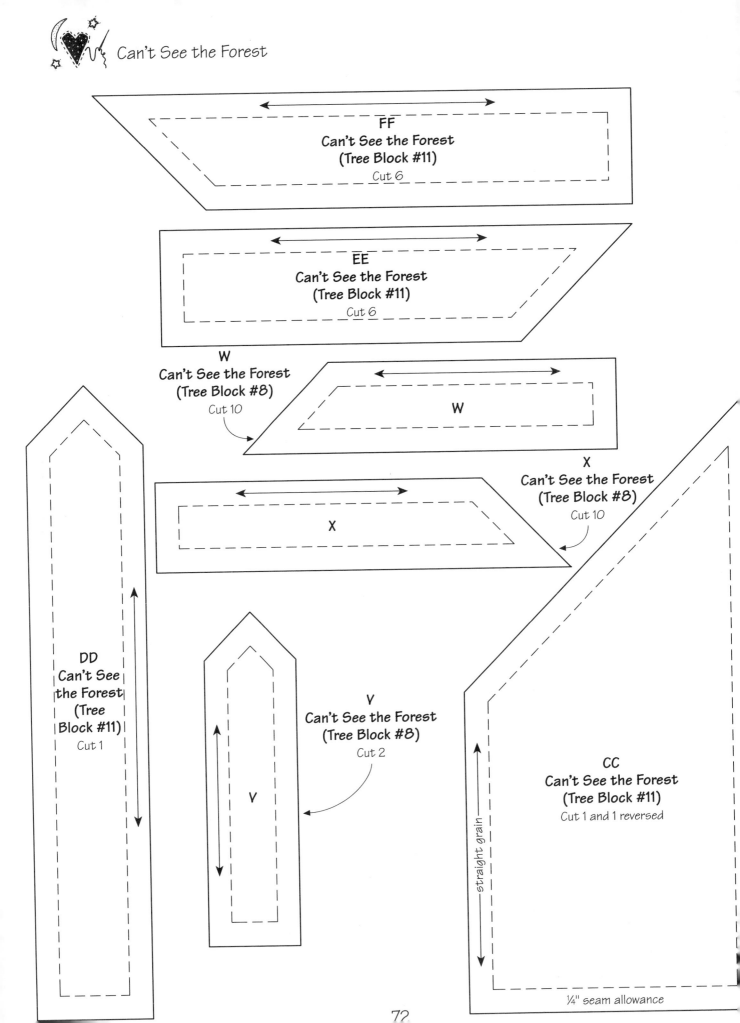

FF
Can't See the Forest
(Tree Block #11)
Cut 6

EE
Can't See the Forest
(Tree Block #11)
Cut 6

W
Can't See the Forest
(Tree Block #8)
Cut 10

W

X
Can't See the Forest
(Tree Block #8)
Cut 10

X

DD
Can't See the Forest
(Tree Block #11)
Cut 1

V
Can't See the Forest
(Tree Block #8)
Cut 2

V

CC
Can't See the Forest
(Tree Block #11)
Cut 1 and 1 reversed

straight grain

¼" seam allowance

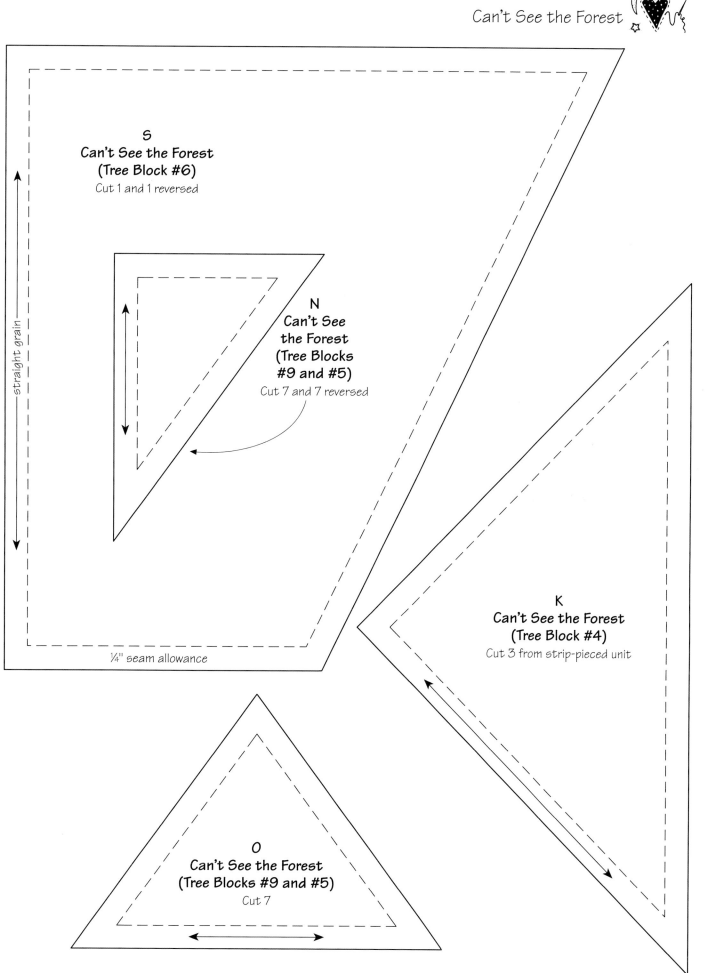

straight grain

S
Can't See the Forest
(Tree Block #6)
Cut 1 and 1 reversed

N
Can't See
the Forest
(Tree Blocks
#9 and #5)
Cut 7 and 7 reversed

¼" seam allowance

K
Can't See the Forest
(Tree Block #4)
Cut 3 from strip-pieced unit

O
Can't See the Forest
(Tree Blocks #9 and #5)
Cut 7

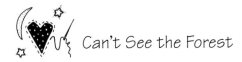

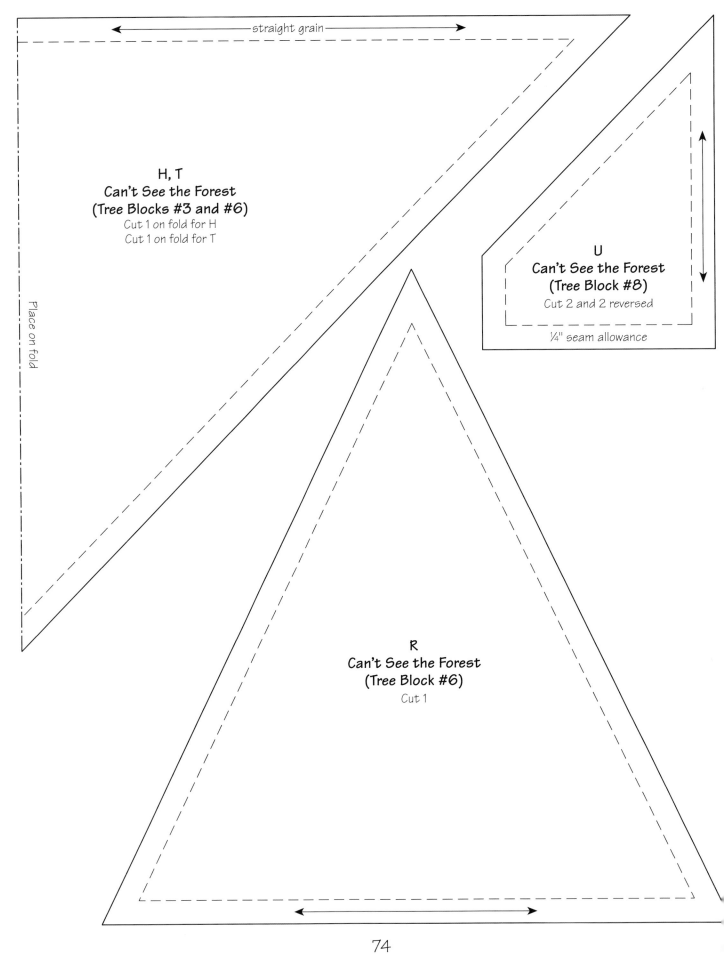

straight grain

Place on fold

H, T
Can't See the Forest
(Tree Blocks #3 and #6)
Cut 1 on fold for H
Cut 1 on fold for T

U
Can't See the Forest
(Tree Block #8)
Cut 2 and 2 reversed

¼" seam allowance

R
Can't See the Forest
(Tree Block #6)
Cut 1

Little Sweethearts & Sweetheart Pockets

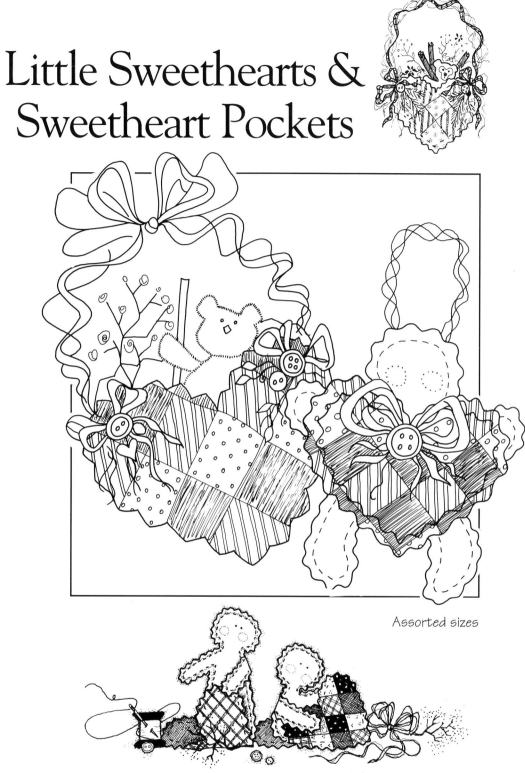

Assorted sizes

Quick and easy to make, Little Sweethearts and the Sweetheart Pockets are delightful gifts. They can decorate your wall, sit on a shelf, or hang as ornaments on your Christmas tree. The Sweetheart Pockets are perfect little containers to display small treasures.

We've made our Little Sweethearts and Sweetheart Pockets from old quilts and linens, too old and worn to salvage. Make your own patchwork or use old linens or old jeans, but be sure to hand or machine quilt it to some batting and a backing. Tea dyeing is a great way to make the pieces look old and more "country." See page 9 for tea-dyeing directions.

All tracing and sewing is done on the right sides of the fabric pieces. This is what makes them so easy to sew and gives them a rustic charm. Patterns are on the pullout pattern insert.

Little Sweethearts

Color photo on page 38.

Materials

1 piece, 5" x 10" of an old quilt, old jeans, or newly made patchwork

12" lengths of raffia, twine, ribbon, or lace for bows

⅛ yd. fabric for doll body

Pink or red stencil paint, colored pencil, crayon, or cosmetic blusher for cheeks

Embellishments: old buttons, lace, jewelry, ribbon, raffia, charms, and dried flowers in any combination

Neutral thread

Small amount of fiberfill stuffing

Tools for both projects

Marking pencil for fabric
Pinking shears
Aluminum foil
Fabric stiffener (Stiffy)
Old brush or sponge to apply stiffener

Directions

1. Trace the body pattern pieces for the Little Sweethearts onto the right side of a doubled piece of body fabric. Leave at least 1" between the traced pieces. Trace the heart pattern on the right side of a doubled piece of quilted fabric.

2. Stitch on the traced lines for the doll body, leaving an opening where indicated for stuffing.

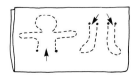

3. With pinking shears, cut the body pieces ¼" away from the stitched line. Stuff the head and hand areas lightly. Stuff the legs to within ½" of the opening. Set aside.

4. With pinking shears, cut the quilted heart piece ¼" from outside the traced line. Sandwich the body pieces inside the hearts and pin in place.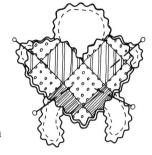

5. For the handle, twist a 12" length of raffia, ribbon, or twine (or a combination) and fold in half to make a loop. Pin loop in place between the back of the doll and the back of the quilted heart.

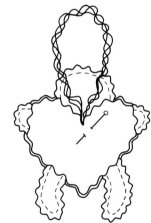

6. Sew the layers together on the traced line, using a zigzag stitch and leaving an opening where indicated. Stuff the heart lightly, then continue to sew the quilted heart closed.
7. Color the doll's cheeks softly.
8. Brush or sponge fabric stiffener on the Little Sweetheart. Lay on a piece of aluminum foil to dry.
9. Glue on an assortment of embellishments.

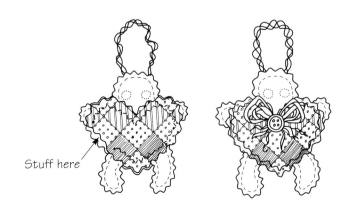

Stuff here

Sweetheart Pockets

Materials

1 piece, 7" x 14" of an old quilt, old jeans, or newly made patchwork

¾ yd. lengths of raffia, twine, lace, or ribbon combined with 3 or 4 strands of raffia for pocket handle

Directions

1. Trace the heart pattern piece onto the right side of a doubled piece of quilted fabric.
2. Stitch around heart pieces on the traced line, leaving an opening where marked.

Open

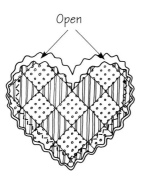

3. Combine ¾ yard lengths of raffia, twine, lace, or ribbon and tie them in a bow.

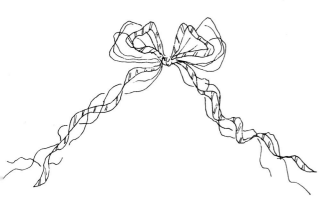

4. Twist the ends of the handle before sewing them on each side of the opening in the Sweetheart Pocket.

5. Brush or sponge fabric stiffener on the inside of the pocket. Crumple aluminum foil into a ball to insert into the pocket while the stiffener dries. Stiffen the outside front, back, and handle. Set aside to dry on a piece of foil.
6. Glue an assortment of embellishments onto the front of the pocket, such as old buttons, lace, charms, old jewelry, dried flowers, and raffia.
7. Stuff the completed pocket with anything that strikes your fancy—flowers, potpourri, cinnamon sticks, an old handkerchief, a little stuffed animal, a special gift, or a treasure. Use your imagination!

Keep thine heart with all diligence; for out of it are the issues of life. Proverbs 4:23

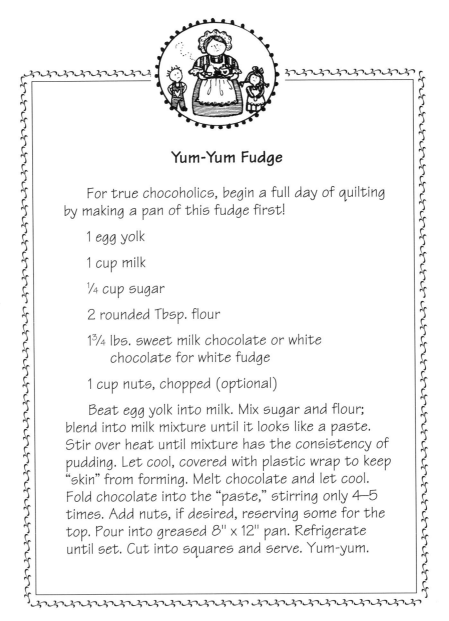

Yum-Yum Fudge

For true chocoholics, begin a full day of quilting by making a pan of this fudge first!

1 egg yolk

1 cup milk

¼ cup sugar

2 rounded Tbsp. flour

1¾ lbs. sweet milk chocolate or white chocolate for white fudge

1 cup nuts, chopped (optional)

Beat egg yolk into milk. Mix sugar and flour; blend into milk mixture until it looks like a paste. Stir over heat until mixture has the consistency of pudding. Let cool, covered with plastic wrap to keep "skin" from forming. Melt chocolate and let cool. Fold chocolate into the "paste," stirring only 4–5 times. Add nuts, if desired, reserving some for the top. Pour into greased 8" x 12" pan. Refrigerate until set. Cut into squares and serve. Yum-yum.

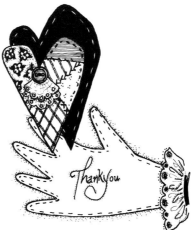

That Patchwork Place Publications and Products

BOOKS

All the Blocks Are Geese by Mary Sue Suit
Angle Antics by Mary Hickey
Animas Quilts by Jackie Robinson
Appliqué Borders: An Added Grace by Jeana Kimball
Baltimore Bouquets by Mimi Dietrich
Basket Garden by Mary Hickey
Biblical Blocks by Rosemary Makhan
Blockbuster Quilts by Margaret J. Miller
Calendar Quilts by Joan Hanson
Cathedral Window: A Fresh Look by Nancy J. Martin
Corners in the Cabin by Paulette Peters
Country Medallion Sampler by Carol Doak
Country Threads by Connie Tesene and Mary Tendall
Easy Machine Paper Piecing by Carol Doak
Even More by Trudie Hughes
Fantasy Flowers: Pieced Flowers for Quilters
    by Doreen Cronkite Burbank
Feathered Star Sampler by Marsha McCloskey
Fit To Be Tied by Judy Hopkins
Five- and Seven-Patch Blocks & Quilts for the ScrapSaver™
    by Judy Hopkins
Four-Patch Blocks & Quilts for the ScrapSaver™
    by Judy Hopkins
Fun with Fat Quarters by Nancy J. Martin
Go Wild with Quilts: 14 North American Birds and Animals
    by Margaret Rolfe
Handmade Quilts by Mimi Dietrich
Happy Endings—Finishing the Edges of Your Quilt
    by Mimi Dietrich
Holiday Happenings by Christal Carter
Home for Christmas by Nancy J. Martin and Sharon Stanley
In The Beginning by Sharon Evans Yenter
Jacket Jazz by Judy Murrah
Lessons in Machine Piecing by Marsha McCloskey
Little By Little: Quilts in Miniature by Mary Hickey
Little Quilts by Alice Berg, Sylvia Johnson, and
    Mary Ellen Von Holt
Lively Little Logs by Donna McConnell
Loving Stitches: A Guide to Fine Hand Quilting
    by Jeana Kimball
More Template-Free™ *Quiltmaking* by Trudie Hughes
Nifty Ninepatches by Carolann M. Palmer
Nine-Patch Blocks & Quilts for the ScrapSaver™
    by Judy Hopkins
Not Just Quilts by Jo Parrott
On to Square Two by Marsha McCloskey
Osage County Quilt Factory by Virginia Robertson
Painless Borders by Sally Schneider
A Perfect Match: A Guide to Precise Machine Piecing
    by Donna Lynn Thomas

Picture Perfect Patchwork by Naomi Norman
Piecemakers® *Country Store* by the Piecemakers
Pineapple Passion by Nancy Smith and Lynda Milligan
A Pioneer Doll and Her Quilts by Mary Hickey
Pioneer Storybook Quilts by Mary Hickey
Quick & Easy Quiltmaking: 26 Projects Featuring Speedy
    Cutting and Piecing Methods by Mary Hickey,
    Nancy J. Martin, Marsha McCloskey & Sara Nephew
Quilts for All Seasons: Year-Round Log Cabin Designs
    by Christal Carter
Quilts for Baby: Easy as A, B, C by Ursula Reikes
Quilts for Kids by Carolann M. Palmer
Quilts from Nature by Joan Colvin
Quilts to Share by Janet Kime
Red and Green: An Appliqué Tradition by Jeana Kimball
Red Wagon Originals by Gerry Kimmel and Linda Brannock
Rotary Riot: 40 Fast & Fabulous Quilts by Judy Hopkins
    and Nancy J. Martin
Rotary Roundup: 40 More Fast & Fabulous Quilts by Judy
    Hopkins and Nancy J. Martin
Round About Quilts by J. Michelle Watts
Samplings from the Sea by Rosemary Makhan
Scrap Happy by Sally Schneider
Sensational Settings: Over 80 Ways to Arrange Your Quilt
    Blocks by Joan Hanson
Sewing on the Line: Fast and Easy Foundation Piecing
    by Lesly-Claire Greenberg
Shortcuts: A Concise Guide to Rotary Cutting
    by Donna Lynn Thomas (metric version available)
Small Talk by Donna Lynn Thomas
Smoothstitch™ *Quilts: Easy Machine Appliqué*
    by Roxi Eppler
The Stitchin' Post by Jean Wells and Lawry Thorn
Strips That Sizzle by Margaret J. Miller
Tea Party Time: Romantic Quilts and Tasty Tidbits
    by Nancy J. Martin
Template-Free™ *Quiltmaking* by Trudie Hughes
Template-Free™ *Quilts and Borders* by Trudie Hughes
Template-Free® *Stars* by Jo Parrott
Watercolor Quilts by Pat Maixner Magaret and
    Donna Ingram Slusser
Women and Their Quilts by Nancyann Johanson Twelker

TOOLS

6" Bias Square®   Rotary Mate™
8" Bias Square®   Rotary Rule™
Metric Bias Square®   Ruby Beholder™
BiRangle™   ScrapSaver™
Pineapple Rule

VIDEO

Shortcuts to America's Best-Loved Quilts

Many titles are available at your local quilt shop. For more information, send $2 for a color catalog to That Patchwork Place, Inc., PO Box 118, Bothell WA 98041-0118 USA.

☎ Call 1-800-426-3126 for the name and location of the quilt shop nearest you.

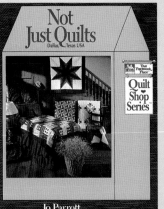